A HISTORICAL READER

Civil
Rights

The African-American Struggle for Equality

nextext

Table of Contents

PART IV: TRAGEDY AND TRIUMPH

*Throughout the reader, vocabulary words appear in boldface
type and are footnoted. Specialized or technical words and phrases
appear in lightface type and are footnoted.*

Life Under Segregation

from

Who Speaks for the Negro?

Recollection of Reverend Joe Carter

BY ROBERT PENN WARREN

Segregation began to appear in the United States after the Civil War (1861–1865). Though slavery had been abolished, laws, known as "Jim Crow laws," began to appear that separated African Americans from white Americans. African Americans were kept from voting and were forced to attend separate schools, use separate stores and restaurants, and to use separate sections on public transport. In 1896, the Supreme Court in the Plessy v. Ferguson decision declared that this policy of "separate but equal" was legal and valid. However, in reality, it was anything but equal. The Plessy decision simply institutionalized racism in the South. In the following selection, the Reverend Joe Carter describes what happened to him when he tried to register to vote in West Feliciana, Louisiana.

Well, I met the CORE[1]—Ruby Livermore, that's his name. And Ronnie Moore. And I met them on a Thursday in August. They explained to me concernen the red-ishen[2] and I told them that I had tried and that I couldn't get none of my neighbors to go with me.

I knew that I was a citizen of the United States and not only our own little parish, because I was fifty-five years old and I had never done anything to go to jail, to be **disenfranchised**,[3] but the state or the parish laws, and through these I did not get to red-ish, and I could hear over the air and on the television they wanted ever citizen to vote. Well, after they explained to me concernen of the vote, you know, which I wanted to do it anyway, and I was glad to lead the people here out of their ig-rance and enlighten them about how to go about it. So I made an agreemint with them how I would go down and ask the Redg-strar, but I tell them that I didn't just want to go by myself. I would like to have somebody to go with me. Well, at that time there was only just me—one—from the West Feliciana Parish. He [Ronnie Moore] said, "Well, Reverend Davis, he wants to red-ish."

So we made an appointmint with him to see Reverend Davis that day, and Reverend Davis sent me word that we would go to Harmon and ask to red-ish, which we did, he made arrangemints for nine o'clock. He was there. Well, a few minutes after because they had a flat, but it wasn't far enough behind the appointmint for me to get disgusted and ignore him. So we went down to the Redg-strar's office, which Ruby and Ronnie wanted to go with us. I told them, no. I would rather to go by myself, you know, go before my people without haven the strangers with us. And they says,

---

[1] CORE—Congress for Racial Equality, group responsible for sponsoring the first sit-ins.

[2] red-ishen—Reverend Carter's way of saying "registration." Throughout the article, spellings represent Reverend Carter's speech style.

[3] **disenfranchised**—deprived of a privilege or a right, especially the right to vote.

"Well, if you-all go down and have any trouble, let us know." Well, they told us where the car would be, which we didn't see the car as they had turned. They were walken. But they told us what type of car they would drive, which was a white car.

When we went in the courthouse we didn't see nobody, we didn't hear nobody. Well, they didn't have any signs you know—"Right," "Left," "Redg-strar's office." Well, we seen the Sher'ff's office, we seen the jury room, and we seen the Circuit office. We had to inquire where was the office, which was with no name on it. We walked around a little and we couldn't find the place and it was some laborers, which were from Boyd, Kirby and from some parish town, and they did some little somethen there and had them in the parish jail and had them worken, on the courthouse there. And Reverend Davis asked the boys, "We looken for the Redg-strar's office." And one of the boys said, "Over yonder." Well, we had already been over there, so that was surely false, and where do our people red-ish to vote—so they couldn't say no more.

Well, there was a white man there. We said, "White folks, can you tell us where the Redg-strar is, please?" He said, "In there." Well, it was two doors, but he just say, "In there"—he didn't tell us no special door. So we turned round and Reverend Davis went back to the Assessor's office and asked him, so he just say, "Up there."

Well, we went on up and I said, "It must be in this hall." The Reverend Davis say to me, he said, "Well, we both can't talk at the same time. And now you just listen and let me talk." Well, we agreed on the outside to do so.

Well, we still didn't see nobody, so when we went down in the little hall to see the Redg-strar's office, I imagine from about here to that wall there—from the main hall—by time we got to the door, just before we got to the door, the Redg-strar, he walked out the door and pulled it behind him and stood in front of the door. Said, "Good mornen, boys, what can I do for you-all?" Well, we spoke to him, "Mornen." So Reverend Davis said, "Well, we come to see if we could red-ish to vote." He said, "Well, I can't appear you now, but you got to bring somethen. You got to show somethen. You got to carry somethen."

Well, Reverend Davis turns, he says, "I really don't know what you mean—by that. You tell me what you mean, probably I can produce what it takes." He said, "Well, you got to go back home and get your two redg-stered voters out of the ward where you live."

Well, at that time the High Sher'ff had come down the hall and standen facen this small hall, that one right there. So Reverend Davis said, "Well, the High Sher'ff knows me, and not only that—all of you knows me here." He says, "Yes, I know they call you Rudolph Davis, but I couldn't swear to it. I couldn't tell it was you upstairs." As I turned, he said then, "Here boy, here boy, you boy." Well, I was looken at the Redg-strar, you see, and I turned around and I said, "You speaken to me?" He said, "Yeah, you come here." So, I turned round and went on back out to him, and when I got out to just about to where he was he walked off down the hall, like he was goen back to the Sher'ff's office, and he had a pencil and a card in his hand. He said, "What's your name?" I said, "Reverend Joe Carter." He attempted to write, but he made one mark. He said, "What's the matter with you fellows? You not satisfied?" I said, "Not exactly." He said, "Well, if you ain't, from now on you will be—you hear?" I said, "Yes sir." He said, "Go back where you come." I turned to go back.

He said, "I ought to lock you up." Well, I didn't say anythen. I just kept walken. Just before I got to the hall, anyway, he said, "I really ought to lock you up." I didn't make him any answer. Then he hollered to the

Deppity, "Grab him, Dan, don't you hear him raisen his voice at me? Consider you're under arrest."

Well, I turned my face to him, you know. And then he searched me—started at my heels and come on up, searchen me. Said, "Take him out there and put handcuffs on him. Lock him up." Then he put my arm down and put it behind me. He said, "Go on out, you." Well, I went on out—take me on out to this car, facen my face across the top of the car, and he reach in with his hands, got his handcuffs—but he still held this left arm behind, and he shook it out of his shackle—and he locked the hand. Well, when I heard the handcuff lock, I just laid the other one back there. They locked me and put me in—told me, "Git in there."

Well, I had pulled my hat off and laid it up on the car. He took my hat and thowed it in the back of the car, where I was, and there was another white man, which the other white young man, when he told [the Deputy] to grab me—they both grabbed me.

Well, I had never been to the jail. I didn't know where the jail-house door was, but I saw a hall and they said, "Go on in there." So I went on up in there and [the Deputy] asked me—he says, "Who's been talken to you?" I said, "Nobody." He said, "You've been over in Clinton, and that damned [racial epithet]—" I said, "I ain't been to no Clinton." "Who been talken to you?" I said, "Nobody been talken to me. Don't you know we got radios and television and I read the papers." I said to him, "The *Journal* says it wants all citizens to red-ish and vote."

So, we're goen on into the jail, and they unlock me, put me in the cell. So they went on back down the hall. They come back about ten minutes later, this young white man, he—I didn't know him—he come back and unlocked the jail cell and told me to come out. So, I come on out and they told me to go on down the hall, so I went on down the hall where there was the little office they had in the jail. When I got in there the Deppity had set up his fixen what he had—so he took my fingerprints first and then he—after he took my fingerprints, then he stood me over side the wall and he take my picture, and after he'd taken my picture, then put me on the scales, took my weight, took my height, and asked me how old I was. So I told him I was fifty-five, three months and five days old today; so after that, he asked me did I have any sisters. I told him yes. I told them I had two daughters— they both live in Scotland, here. And, I had to give my oldest daughter's house number, as far as street and 1740. My baby girl had just moved and I hadn't been there to the new house and I couldn't give them their number, but I told them she's in Scotland.

They take me on back, but when they was unlocken the cell—see, I had my clothes, my hat. Then the High Sher'ff, Mr. Percy, he come in the hall. He said, "Take his hat from him. He don't need nothen." So they took my hat. So he said, "Search him agin." So they searched me over—said, "Take all his clothes. He don't need nothen, nohow." So they went back there and got a uniform and then they made me pull all my clothes off. They given me the uniform. "Put him," he says to the Deppity, "put him under that shower." Says, "Get him a shower—he's musty—stinks." So, I didn't say anything. I didn't say anything to him. He says, "Who been talken to you?" I said, "Nobody." He said, "You ain't goen to tell me, huh?" I said, "Well, I ain't got nothen to tell you."

I put that coverall on and they went on in.

They sent me my dinner down, and no spoon to eat with. They had a spoon up in the grates up there. I don't know how long it had been up there. The man brought me my dinner, he said, "Get that spoon up yonder and eat, you." So I say, "I don't need it because I don't eat this." But I just expect they don't own a garbage can. Well, I stayed in that jail from about nine thirty till two thirty without water. Their faucet was broke and you could get water out of it, but I didn't know—you see, I had to put all my weight up on it to get the water on—and then when I get it on I had to do the same thing to get it off, but I thought it was broke all the time because the threads were stripped on it. So anyway, the wardman, he told me how to get the water on and how to get it off.

About nine thirty or a quarter to ten that night, they came back—somebody has got money from somewhere. I don't know where they got it from, but they come in that night and call me to get up, come on and get out of there. Well, I got up and they give me my clothes and I pulled the coveralls off and come back in the office—and had to sign a bond—and had to sign that I had gotten my car back, with all my papers, which I didn't get them all because I had a test paper there that Ruby and Ronnie had give me, you see, before I went in there to red-ish, I let them know that I did understand how to fill out the redg-stration blank. Well, I had that up over my sun glare—of my car—but I had signed a paper that I had my car back in good standen, but I was still in jail. I didn't know whether wheels was on my car, but I had to sign it because they had me in jail and I couldn't get out to see the car.

Well, when I did get out I reached over there, before I got in my car, and my paper was gone. So, I didn't say anything. Well, Ruby, he got in the car with me and he asked me if I got harmed. He said, "Well, check the car and see if you got the paper." Well, I said, "No, I don't have my redg-stration papers." But, you see, by being a minister, I always carry my Bible, my Psalm Book, and my Pastor's Guide. I keeps that in the car. Any time you see the car, you see that—with a coat. Care how hot it is—I always carry the coat, because lots of times I be caught up the road for—have to bury some baby or somethen, and I keep those books with me.

Well, I went in the car and they didn't take nothen but them test papers. That's all they took from me. So, after I got home, well, I had a bunch of people there, waiten for me. When I got home, my wife said, "Joe, you oughtn't have went down there." She said, "Now, if you go back down, I'm going to leave you." I said, "Well, you can get your clothes and start now, because I'm going back." So I say, "I'm on my way back tomorrow."

QUESTIONS TO CONSIDER

1. Why does the sheriff throw Reverend Carter in jail? What is Carter's "crime"?

2. What words would you use to describe Carter?

3. Why do you think Carter decides to return to the courthouse the following day?

Segregation Reconsidered

BY THE PRESIDENT'S COMMITTEE ON CIVIL RIGHTS

Opposition to segregation grew rapidly in the twentieth century. In 1910, the National Association for the Advancement of Colored People (NAACP) was founded to fight against lynching and discrimination. World War II greatly accelerated the breaking down of discrimination. More than 700,000 African Americans served in the armed forces during the war, and in 1948, belatedly, President Truman ended segregation in the army. Two years earlier, Truman had established a Committee on Civil Rights. Its report, To Secure These Rights, *was a blistering critique of the failure of the nation to defend the civil rights of its minorities, and it called upon the government to take an active role in fighting racial discrimination. The following selection from the report describes life under segregation.*

The "Separate But Equal" Failure

Mention has already been made of the "separate but equal" policy of the southern states by which Negroes are said to be entitled to the same public service as whites but on a strictly **segregated**[1] basis. The theory behind this policy is complex. On one hand, it recognizes Negroes as citizens and as intelligent human beings entitled to enjoy the status accorded the individual in our American heritage of freedom. It theoretically gives them access to all the rights, privileges, and services of a civilized, democratic society. On the other hand, it brands the Negro with the mark of inferiority and asserts that he is not fit to associate with white people.

Legally enforced segregation has been followed throughout the South since the close of the Reconstruction [post–Civil War] era. In these states it is generally illegal for Negroes to attend the same schools as whites; attend theaters patronized by whites; visit parks where whites relax; eat, sleep or meet in hotels, restaurants, or public halls frequented by whites. This is only a partial enumeration—legally imposed separation of races has become highly refined. In the eyes of the law, it is also an offense for whites to attend "Negro" schools, theaters and similar places. The result has been the familiar system of racial segregation in both public and private institutions which cuts across the daily lives of southern citizens from the cradle to the grave.

Legally-enforced segregation has been largely limited to the South. But segregation is also widely prevalent in the North, particularly in housing, and in hotel and restaurant accommodations. Segregation has not been enforced by states alone. The federal government has tolerated it even where it has full authority to eliminate it. . . .

---

[1] **segregated**—separated or divided based on race.

The Fourteenth Amendment forbids a state to deny "to any person within its jurisdiction the equal protection of the laws." Moreover, the general spirit of the three Civil War Amendments[2] seems to guarantee to all persons a full and equal status in American society.

Yet the Supreme Court, beginning with its decision in *Plessy v. Ferguson,* in 1896, has approved state legislation requiring segregation between Negroes and whites on the theory that segregation, as such, is not discriminatory. The Court dismissed the contention that "the enforced separation of the two races stamps the colored race with a badge of inferiority," and observed, "if this be so, it is not by reason of anything found in the act, but solely because the colored race chooses to put that construction upon it." So long as laws requiring segregation do not establish unequal facilities, the legal doctrine holds, there is no unreasonable discrimination and therefore no denial of equal protection under the law.

This judicial legalization of segregation was not accomplished without protest. Justice Harlan, a Kentuckian, in one of the most vigorous and forthright dissenting opinions in Supreme Court history, denounced his colleagues for the manner in which they interpreted away the substance of the Thirteenth and Fourteenth Amendments. In his dissent in the *Plessy* case, he said:

> Our Constitution is color blind, and neither knows nor tolerates classes among citizens. . . . We boast of the freedom enjoyed by our people above all other peoples. But it is difficult to reconcile that boast with a state of the law which, practically, puts the brand of servitude and degradation upon a large class of our fellow citizens, our equals before the law. The thin

---

[2] three Civil War Amendments—Amendments Thirteen, Fourteen, and Fifteen. Amendment Thirteen ended slavery in the United States; Amendment Fourteen defines citizenship and extends it to African Americans; Amendment Fifteen guarantees the right to vote.

disguise of "equal" accommodations . . . will not mislead anyone, or **atone**[3] for the wrong this day done.

If evidence beyond that of **dispassionate**[4] reason was needed to justify Justice Harlan's statement, history has provided it. Segregation has become the cornerstone of the elaborate structure of discrimination against some American citizens. Theoretically this system simply duplicates educational, recreational and other public services, according facilities to the two races which are "separate but equal." In the Committee's opinion this is one of the outstanding myths of American history for it is almost always true that while indeed separate, these facilities are far from equal. Throughout the segregated public institutions, Negroes have been denied an equal share of tax-supported services and facilities. So far as private institutions are concerned, there is no specific legal disability on the right of Negroes to develop equal institutions of their own. However, the economic, social, and indirect legal obstacles to this course are staggering.

Following the *Plessy* decision, the Supreme Court for many years enforced with a degree of leniency the rule that segregated facilities must be equal. Gradually, however, the Court became stricter about requiring a showing of equality. During the last decade, in line with its vigorous defense of civil rights generally, the Court has been particularly insistent upon adherence to the "equal" part of the separate but equal rule. In 1938, in *Missouri ex rel. Gaines v. Canada,* it held that Missouri might not fulfill its obligation under the rule by offering to pay the tuition of a Negro resident of Missouri at an out-of-state law school in lieu of permitting him to attend the law school at the University of Missouri.

---

[3] **atone**—make amends, as for a sin or fault.

[4] **dispassionate**—fair; not influenced by personal or emotional involvement.

The Court laid down the plain rule that if a state chooses to provide within its borders specialized educational facilities for citizens of one race, it must make similar provision, also within its borders, for citizens of other races.

This insistence upon equal facilities is encouraging. Experience requires the prediction, however, that the degree of equality will never be complete, and never certain. In any event we believe that not even the most mathematically precise equality of segregated institutions can properly be considered equality under the law. No argument or rationalization can alter this basic fact: a law which forbids a group of American citizens to associate with other citizens in the ordinary course of daily living creates inequality by imposing a caste status[5] on the minority group.

---

[5] caste status—social class position; meaning that this kind of law creates inequality by forcing members of the minority group into a subclass of society.

QUESTIONS TO CONSIDER

1. According to the report, in what ways was widespread segregation practiced in the South, and, to a lesser extent, in the North?

2. In what ways does segregation violate the spirit of the Civil War Amendments?

3. Can segregated facilities and services be completely equal? Explain your answer.

from

Coming of Age in Mississippi

BY ANNE MOODY

*Anne Moody was born in 1940 in Centreville, Mississippi. Her
parents were sharecroppers—they worked a plot of land for a white
man, who shared half the proceeds from the sale of the crops with
them. The Moodys were desperately poor, and at age nine, Anne
went to work as a maid, while still attending school. Anne's life was
radically changed in 1955 when Emmet Till, a young African
American visiting Mississippi from Chicago, was murdered by white
men for speaking to a white woman who ran a drugstore. Anne
became suddenly aware of the brutality of the segregated South.
The following selection from her autobiography* Coming of Age in
Mississippi *describes the violence that shadowed African Americans
in the South.*

I was fifteen years old when I began to hate people.
I hated the white men who murdered Emmet Till and I
hated all the other whites who were responsible for the
countless murders Mrs. Rice had told me about and

those I vaguely remembered from childhood. But I also hated Negroes. I hated them for not standing up and doing something about the murders. In fact, I think I had a stronger resentment toward Negroes for letting the whites kill them than toward the whites. Anyway, it was at this stage in my life that I began to look upon Negro men as cowards. I could not respect them for smiling in a white man's face, addressing him as Mr. So-and-So, saying yessuh and nossuh when after they were home behind closed doors that same white man was a [expletive] or any other name more suitable than mister. . . .

One day, a rumor was spread throughout town that a Negro had been making telephone calls to a white operator and threatening to molest her. It was also said that the calls had been traced to a certain phone that was now under watch.

Next thing we heard in the Negro community was that they had caught and nearly beaten to death a boy who, they said, had made the calls to the white operator. All the Negroes went around saying, "Y'all know that boy didn't do that." "That boy" was my classmate Jerry. A few months later I got a chance to talk to him and he told me what happened.

He said he had used the telephone at Billups and Fillups service station and was on his way home when Sheriff Ed Cassidy came along in his pickup truck.

"Hey, buddy," Cassidy called, "you on your way home?"

"Yes," Jerry answered.

"Jump in, I'm goin' your way, I'll give you a lift."

Then Jerry told me that when they got out there by the scales where the big trucks weigh at the old camp intersection, Cassidy let him out, telling him that he had forgotten something in town and had to go back and pick it up. At that point, Jerry told me, he didn't suspect anything. He just got out of the truck and told Cassidy thanks. But as soon as the sheriff pulled away, a car came along and stopped. There were four men in it. A deep voice ordered Jerry to get into the car. When he saw that two of the men were Jim Dixon and Nat Withers, whom he had often seen hanging around town with Cassidy, he started to run. But the two in the back jumped out and grabbed him. They forced him into the car and drove out into the camp area. When they got about five miles out, they turned down a little dark dirt road, heavily shaded with trees. They pushed Jerry out of the car onto the ground. He got up and dashed into the woods but they caught up with him and dragged him farther into the woods. Then they tied him to a tree and beat him with a big thick leather strap and a piece of hose pipe.

I asked him if they told him why they were beating him.

"No, not at first," Jerry said, "but when I started screamin' and cryin' and askin' them why they were beatin' me Dixon told me I was tryin' to be smart and they just kept on beatin' me. Then one of the men I didn't know asked me, 'Did you make that phone call, boy?' I said no. I think he kinda believed me cause he stopped beatin' me but the others didn't. The rest of them beat me until I passed out. When I came out of it I was lying on the ground, untied, naked and bleeding. I tried to get up but I was hurtin' all over and it was hard to move. Finally I got my clothes on that them [expletive] had tore offa me and I made it out to the main highway, but I fainted again. When I woke up I was home in bed.

"Daddy and them was scared to take me to the hospital in Centreville. I didn't even see a doctor 'cause they were scared to take me to them white doctors. Wasn't any bones or anything broken. I was swollen all over, though. And you can see I still have bruises and cuts from the strap, but otherwise I guess I'm O.K."

When I asked him whether they were going to do anything about it, he said that his daddy had gotten a white lawyer from Baton Rouge. But after the lawyer pried around in Centreville for a few days, he suddenly disappeared.

Jerry's beating shook up all the Negroes in town. But the most shocking and unjust crime of all occurred a few months later, about two weeks before school ended.

One night, about one o'clock, I was awakened by what I thought was a terrible nightmare. It was an empty dream that consisted only of hollering and screaming voices. It seemed as though I was in an empty valley screaming. And the sounds of my voice were reflected in a million echoes that were so loud I was being lifted in mid-air by the sound waves. I found myself standing trembling in the middle of the floor reaching for the light string. Then I saw Mama running to the kitchen, in her nightgown.

"Mama! Mama! What's all them voices? Where're all those people? What's happening?"

"I don't know," she said, coming to my bedroom door.

"Listen! Listen!" I said, almost screaming.

"Stop all that loud talking fo' you wake up the rest of them chaps. It must be a house on fire or somethin' 'cause of all the screamin'. Somebody must be hurt in it or somethin' too. Ray is getting the car, we gonna go see what it is," she said and headed for the back door.

"You going in your gown?" I asked her.

"We ain't gonna git out of the car. Come on, you can go," she said. "But don't slam the door and wake them chaps up."

I followed her out of the back door in my pajamas. Raymond was just backing the car out of the driveway.

When we turned the corner leaving the quarters, Raymond drove slowly alongside hundreds of people running down the road. They were all headed in the direction of the blaze that reddened the sky.

The crowd of people began to swell until driving was utterly impossible. Finally the long line of cars stopped. We were about two blocks away from the burning house now. The air was so hot that water was running down the faces of the people who ran past the car. The burning house was on the rock road, leading to the school, adjacent to the street we stopped on. So we couldn't tell which house it was. From where we sat, it seemed as though it could have been two or three of them burning. I knew every Negro living in the houses that lined that rock road. I passed them every day on my way to and from school.

I sat there in my pajamas, wishing I had thrown on a dress or something so I could get out of the car.

"Ray, ask somebody who house it is," Mama said to Raymond.

"Hi! Excuse me." Raymond leaned out of the car and spoke to a Negro man. "Do you know who house is on fire?"

"I heard it was the Taplin family. They say the whole family is still in the house. Look like they are done for, so they say."

Didn't any one of us say anything after that. We just sat in the car silently. I couldn't believe what the man had just said. "A whole family burned to death—impossible!" I thought.

"What you think happened, Ray?" Mama finally said to Raymond.

"I don't know. You never kin tell," Raymond said. "It seems mighty strange, though."

Soon people started walking back down the road. The screams and hollering had stopped. People were almost whispering now. They were all Negroes, although I was almost sure I had seen some whites pass before. "I guess not," I thought, sitting there sick inside. Some of the ladies passing the car had tears running down their faces, as they whispered to each other.

"Didn't you smell that gasoline?" I heard a lady who lived in the quarters say.

"That house didn't just catch on fire. And just think them [expletive] burned up a whole family," another lady said. Then they were quiet again.

Soon their husbands neared the car.

"Heh, Jones," Raymond said to one of the men. "How many was killed?"

"About eight or nine of them, Ray. They say the old lady and one of the children got out. I didn't see her nowhere, though."

"You think the house was set on fire?" Raymond asked.

"It sho' looks like it, Ray. It burned down like nothing. When I got there that house was burning on every side. If it had started on the inside of the house at some one place then it wouldn't burn down like it did. All the walls fell in together. Too many strange things are happening round here these days."

Now most of the people and cars were gone, Raymond drove up to the little rock road and parked. I almost vomited when I caught a whiff of the odor of burned bodies mixed with the gasoline. The wooden frame house had been burned to ashes. All that was left were some iron bedposts and springs, a blackened refrigerator, a stove, and some kitchen equipment.

We sat in the car for about an hour, silently looking at this debris and the ashes that covered the nine charcoal-burned bodies. A hundred or more also stood around— Negroes from the neighborhood in their pajamas, night-gowns, and housecoats and even a few whites, with their eyes fixed on that dreadful scene. I shall never forget the expressions on the faces of the Negroes. There was almost **unanimous**[1] hopelessness in them. The still, sad faces watched the smoke rising from the remains until the smoke died down to practically nothing. There was

---

[1] **unanimous**—the quality or state of being in agreement.

something strange about that smoke. It was the thickest and blackest smoke I had ever seen.

Raymond finally drove away, but it was impossible for him to take me away from that nightmare. Those screams, those faces, that smoke, would never leave me.

The next day I took the long, roundabout way to school. I didn't want to go by the scene that was so fixed in my mind. I tried to convince myself that nothing had happened in the night. And I wanted so much to believe that, to believe anything but the dream itself. However, at school, everybody was talking about it. All during each class there was whispering from student to student. Hadn't many of my classmates witnessed the burning last night. I wished they had. If so, they wouldn't be talking so much, I thought. Because I had seen it, and I couldn't talk about it. I just couldn't.

I was so glad when the bell sounded for the lunch hour. I picked up my books and headed home. I couldn't endure another minute of that torture. I was in such a hurry to get away from the talk at school I forgot to take the roundabout way home. Before I realized it, I was standing there where the Taplins' house had been. It looked quite different by day than it had at night. The ashes and junk had been scattered as if someone had looked for the remains of the bodies. The heavy black smoke had disappeared completely. But I stood there looking at the spot where I had seen it rising and I saw it again, slowly drifting away, disappearing before my eyes. I tore myself away and ran almost all the way home.

When I walked in the house Mama didn't even ask me why I came home. She just looked at me. And for the first time I realized she understood what was going on within me, or was trying to anyway. I took two aspirins and went to bed. I stayed there all afternoon. When it was time for me to go to work after school, Mama didn't come in. She must have known I wasn't in the mood for

Mrs. Burke that evening. I wasn't in the mood for anything. I was just there inside of myself, inflicting pain with every thought that ran through my mind.

That night Centreville was like a ghost town. It was so quiet and still. The quietness almost drove me crazy. It was too quiet for sleeping that night, yet it was too restless for dreams and too dry for weeping.

A few days later, it was reported that the fire had started from the kerosene lamp used by Mrs. Taplin as a light for the new baby. Nobody bought that story. At least none of those who witnessed that fire and smelled all that gasoline. They were sure that more than a lampful of kerosene caused that house to burn that fast.

There was so much doubt and **dissension**[2] about the Taplin burning that finally FBI agents arrived on the scene and quietly conducted an investigation. But as usual in this sort of case, the investigation was dropped as soon as public interest died down.

Months later the story behind the burning was whispered throughout the Negro community. Some of the Taplins' neighbors who had been questioned put their scraps of information together and came up with an answer that made sense:

Living next door to the Taplin family was a Mr. Banks, a high yellow mulatto[3] man of much wealth. He was a bachelor with land and cattle galore. He had for some time discreetly taken care of a white woman, the mother of three whose husband had deserted her, leaving her to care for the children the best way she knew how. She lived in a bottom where a few other poor whites lived. The Guild during one of its investigations discovered the children at home alone one night—and many other nights after that. Naturally, they wondered

---

[2] **dissension**—disagreement.

[3] mulatto—a person of mixed white and black ancestry.

where the mother was spending her nights. A few days' observation of the bottom proved she was leaving home, after putting the children to bed, and being picked up by Mr. Banks in **inconspicuous**[4] places.

When the Taplin family was burned, Mr. Banks escaped his punishment. Very soon afterward he locked his house and disappeared. And so did the white lady from the bottom.

I could barely wait until school was out. I was so sick of Centreville. I made up my mind to tell Mama I had to get away, if only for the summer. I had thought of going to Baton Rouge to live with my Uncle Ed who was now married and living there with his family.

A few days before school ended I sat in the midst of about six of my classmates who insisted on discussing the Taplin family. By the time I got home, my nerves were in shreds from thinking of some of the things they had said. I put my books down, took two aspirins, and got into bed. I didn't think I could go to work that evening because I was too nervous to be around Mrs. Burke. I had not been myself at work since the Emmet Till murder, especially after the way Mrs. Burke had talked to me about the Taplin family. But she had become more observant of my reactions.

"What's wrong with you? Is you sick?" Mama asked me.

I didn't answer her.

"Take your shoes off that spread. You better git up and go to work. Mrs. Burke gonna fire you."

"I got a headache and I don't feel like going," I said.

"What's wrong with you, getting so many headaches around here?"

I decided not to wait any longer to tell Mama my plan.

"Mama, I am gonna write Ed and see can I stay with him this summer and get a job in Baton Rouge. I am just

---

[4] **inconspicuous**—not readily noticeable.

tired of working for Mrs. Burke for a dollar a day. I can make five dollars a day in Baton Rouge and I make only six dollars a week here."

"Ed them ain't got enough room for you to live with them. Take your shoes off," Mama said, and left me lying in bed.

As soon as she left, I got up and wrote my letter. About five days later I received an answer from Ed. He said I was welcome, so I started packing to leave the next day. Mama looked at me as if she didn't want me to go. But she knew better than to ask me.

I was fifteen years old and leaving home for the first time. I wasn't even sure I could get a job at that age. But I had to go anyway, if only to breathe a slightly different atmosphere. I was choking to death in Centreville. I couldn't go on working for Mrs. Burke pretending I was dumb and innocent, pretending I didn't know what was going on in all her Guild meetings, or about Jerry's beating, or about the Taplin burning, and everything else that was going on. I was sick of pretending, sick of selling my feelings for a dollar a day.

QUESTIONS TO CONSIDER

1. Why was Anne Moody upset by the way African Americans reacted to the murders?

2. For what reason was Jerry beaten? Why was the Taplin house burned?

3. Why does Anne Moody want to go away to Baton Rouge?

School Segregation Challenged

In 1954, the Supreme Court took a major step in desegregating the South. In the case of Brown v. Board of Education of Topeka, the Court ruled that "Separate educational facilities are inherently unequal." The case had been brought by the lawyers of the NAACP led by Thurgood Marshall (1908–1993), who would go on to become the first African-American Supreme Court Justice. Still, despite the obvious importance of the Brown decision, enforcement of the Court's ruling was to prove anything but easy. As the NAACP lawyer Charles Houston said, "Nobody needs to explain to a Negro the difference between the law in the books and the law in action." The following selection is an excerpt from the unanimous opinion of the Court in the Brown case and some memoirs of Marshall and his legal team.

from *Brown v. Board of Education*

Chief Justice Earl Warren delivered the opinion of the Court.

These cases come to us from the States of Kansas, South Carolina, Virginia, and Delaware. They are premised on different facts and different local conditions, but a common legal question justifies their consideration together in this consolidated opinion.

In each of the cases, minors of the Negro race, through their legal representatives, seek the aid of the courts in obtaining admission to the public schools of their community on a nonsegregated basis. In each instance, they had been denied admission to schools attended by white children under laws requiring or permitting segregation according to race. This segregation was alleged to deprive the **plaintiffs**[1] of the equal protection of the laws under the Fourteenth Amendment. . . .

In approaching this problem, we cannot turn the clock back to 1868, when the Amendment was adopted, or even to 1896 when *Plessy v. Ferguson* was written. We must consider public education in the light of its full development and its present place in American life throughout the nation. Only in this way can it be determined if segregation in public schools deprives these plaintiffs of the equal protection of the laws.

Today, education is perhaps the most important function of state and local governments. **Compulsory**[2] school attendance laws and the great expenditures for education both demonstrate our recognition of the importance of education to our democratic society. It is required in the performance of our most basic public responsibilities, even service in the armed forces. It is the very foundation of good citizenship. Today it is a

---

[1] **plaintiffs**—those who file suit.

[2] **compulsory**—enforced; mandatory.

principal instrument in awakening the child to cultural values, in preparing him for later professional training, and in helping him to adjust normally to his environment. In these days, it is doubtful that any child may reasonably be expected to succeed in life if he is denied the opportunity of an education. Such an opportunity, where the state has undertaken to provide it, is a right which must be made available to all on equal terms.

We come then to the question presented: Does segregation of children in public schools solely on the basis of race, even though the physical facilities and other **"tangible"**[3] factors may be equal, deprive the children of the minority group of equal educational opportunities? We believe that it does.

In *Sweatt v. Painter*, in finding that a segregated law school for Negroes could not provide them equal educational opportunities, this Court relied in large part on "those qualities which are incapable of objective measurement but which make for greatness in a law school." In *McLaurin v. Oklahoma State Regents*, the Court, in requiring that a Negro admitted to a white graduate school be treated like all other students, again resorted to intangible considerations: ". . . his ability to study, to engage in discussions and exchange views with other students, and, in general, to learn his profession." Such considerations apply with added force to children in grade and high schools. To separate them from others of similar age and qualifications solely because of their race generates a feeling of inferiority as to their status in the community that may affect their hearts and minds in a way unlikely ever to be undone. The effect of this separation on their educational opportunities was well stated by a finding in the Kansas case by a court which nevertheless felt compelled to rule against the Negro plaintiffs:

---

[3] **tangible**—capable of being identified and assessed at a certain value.

"Segregation of white and colored children in public schools has a detrimental effect upon the colored children. The impact is greater when it has the **sanction**[4] of the law; for the policy of separating the races is usually interpreted as denoting the inferiority of the Negro group. A sense of inferiority affects the motivation of a child to learn. Segregation with the sanction of law, therefore, has a tendency to retard the educational and mental development of Negro children and to deprive them of some of the benefits they would receive in a racially integrated school system."

Whatever may have been the extent of psychological knowledge at the time of *Plessy v. Ferguson*, this finding is amply supported by modern authority. Any language in *Plessy v. Ferguson* contrary to this finding is rejected.

We conclude that in the field of public education the doctrine of "separate but equal" has no place. Separate educational facilities are inherently unequal.

May 17, 1954

from *Thurgood Marshall: Justice For All*
edited by Roger L. Goldman

Marshall's greatest victory came in 1954, when he led the legal team that challenged school segregation before the Warren court. As the case progressed, three secret dramas unfolded.

First, Marshall heard that President Eisenhower had pressured Chief Justice Earl Warren to retain school segregation. Marshall says that Ralph Bunche, former U.S. undersecretary to the United Nations, told him that at a

---

[4] **sanction**—formal or authoritative approval.

White House dinner he heard Warren tell Eisenhower off in no uncertain terms: "I thought I would never have to say this to you, but I now find it necessary to say to you specifically: You mind your business, and I'll mind mine." Later, Marshall said Eisenhower's attempt to pressure Warren was the "most **despicable**[5] job any president has done in my life."

Second was Marshall's mental combat with Justice Felix Frankfurter. Throughout the case, the justice had peppered him with questions. At one point, just before recessing for the day, Frankfurter asked him if the case would be affected if the 14th Amendment to the Constitution had not been intended to end segregation. "My God, the light went on, which meant you had to come back in the morning," recalls William T. Coleman, who worked with Marshall on the case. "Well, from 5 o'clock until 7 o'clock in the morning—the work that went into how do you answer that question!"

Later, Marshall discovered that it was Frankfurter who had put the phrase "all deliberate speed" into the decision, creating a loophole that allowed segregationists to delay the integration of schools instead of immediately obeying the court order. . . .

The third drama involved Justice Stanley Reed, a Kentuckian. Marshall had been told that Reed had independently hired a clerk to write a dissent to the opinion. In Marshall's mind, the question was: How many justices will join in Reed's dissent?

As the decision came down, Marshall was watching Reed's eyes. "When Warren read the opinion," he says, Reed "looked me right straight in the face the whole time because he wanted to see what happened when I realized that he didn't write that dissent. I was looking right straight at him, and I did like that [a nod of the

___
[5] **despicable**—worthy of moral indignation.

head], and he did like that [a nod in response]." The decision was unanimous.

Marshall would later comment that the *Brown* decision "probably did more than anything else to awaken the Negro from his **apathy**[6] to demanding his right to equality."

* * *

Paul Gewirtz, now a professor of law at Yale University, clerked for Thurgood Marshall during the 1971 term. In this essay, which originally appeared in The Yale Law Journal *(November 1991), Professor Gewirtz pays tribute to Marshall's accomplishments as a lawyer and judge and provides insight into his wonderfully human character.*

Thurgood Marshall's life as a civil rights lawyer inspired my decision to go to law school, so it was the greatest of dreams fulfilled when I came to work as his law clerk at the Supreme Court. Now, as he leaves the Court, it is an honor to mark his retirement in these pages.

Marshall is an extraordinary figure in American legal history. He has lived many lives—indeed, while others marvel over his professional durability at the age of eighty-three, I actually think of him as having compressed more than a hundred years of living into that time span. He was the country's greatest civil rights lawyer during the greatest period for civil rights advances in our history, and in that role he lived a life of relentless intensity and danger, and one of transforming achievement. He was a United States Court of Appeals Judge. He was Solicitor General of the United States (his favorite job, he has often said with complete seriousness—an advocate's job in which he spoke for "the United States," not simply a faction or **insurgent**[7] part of the whole). Finally, he became a Justice on the

---

[6] **apathy**—indifference; lack of interest or concern.

[7] **insurgent**—rebellious.

Supreme Court of the United States during one of its most dramatic periods of change. While he was a top government official for much of this time—an insider and a colleague of the advantaged—he spent his entire career trying to protect the disadvantaged and identifying with them.

The centerpiece of his public life is and always will be *Brown v. Board of Education.* Marshall did not win *Brown* alone, and never claimed to have done so, but he was the guiding force and justly became the symbol of the triumph. Much has been written about the long litigation campaign leading to the Supreme Court's unanimous decision in *Brown.* But one aspect of Marshall's achievement is rarely emphasized: to do what he did required an heroic imagination. He grew up in a ruthlessly discriminatory world—a world in which segregation of the races was pervasive and taken for granted, where lynching was common, where the black man's inherent inferiority was proclaimed widely and wantonly. Thurgood Marshall had the capacity to imagine a radically different world, the imaginative capacity to believe that such a world was possible, the strength to sustain that image in the mind's eye and the heart's longing, and the courage and ability to make that imagined world real. The **predicate**[8] for the great achievement of *Brown* was to imagine something better than the present—to resist the **acquiescence**,[9] passivity, fear, and accommodation that overcome so many, to defy an insistent reality with imagination and then to fight for what was imagined.

Brown changed the world. And because of that, Thurgood Marshall's life stands for the idea that law can change the world and that the Supreme Court can be a powerful force in fulfilling our best public values. That

---

[8] **predicate**—base; foundation.

[9] **acquiescence**—tendency to accept.

was what drew me to the law, and what has drawn so many others. *Brown*, then, is not just a case; its importance cannot be assessed just by totaling up what ending enforced school segregation may have accomplished. Its importance cannot be assessed even by recognizing that it gave broad legitimacy to the modern political struggle for racial equality. Its broadest importance is its embodiment of a conception of law and of the courts.

The naming of Thurgood Marshall to the Supreme Court, therefore, was an act of the greatest importance. His becoming a part of the Court showed how much he had changed the world—in many ways it was the most striking indication of the transformation he had wrought. For all of his imaginative heroism, it is hard to believe that in the 1930's, '40's and '50's Marshall ever imagined that he might someday sit on the Court, be more than an insurgent advocate waiting for others—the Justices—to vindicate him. He created the world that made his own ultimate personal triumph possible. He would now share the power to decide. His becoming a Justice became part of what *Brown* meant.

The perspective he brought to the Court was unique. The other Justices had diverse life experiences, and many were major public figures in their own right. But Marshall brought something distinctive to the Court. The distinctiveness was not simply that he was the first black to sit on the Court, but that he had spent much of his professional life working among the oppressed and the insurgent. To be sure, by the time Marshall came to the Supreme Court he knew more Presidents and Congressmen than most Justices, and he knew their needs and their weaknesses; indeed, they were the subject of many of his best stories. But Marshall also knew the other side of the tracks, not simply as an observer but as one who had called it home; and he always thought of himself as an activist on its behalf. He brought to the Court a sense of how the world worked, and how it worked against those at the bottom. He knew what police stations were like, what rural Southern life was like, what the New York streets were like, what trial courts were like, what hard-nosed local political campaigns were like, what death sentences were like, and what being black in America was like and he knew what it felt like to be at risk as a human being. Most importantly, perhaps, he knew the difference that law could make in all those places. None of his experiences with the harshness of life made him bitter or cynical about law's possibilities. He knew well how law could trample individuals, but he remained faithful to an ideal of what it could do to protect individuals.

QUESTIONS TO CONSIDER

1. What was the Supreme Court's decision in *Brown v. Board of Education*?

2. What are some of the educational "intangibles" that the Justices deem so important?

3. According to Justice Thurgood Marshall, what effect did the *Brown v. Board of Education* decision have on African Americans in general?

A Segregated America

▲
African-American students trying to get an education in the segregated South.

◀ **African-American School** Students stand before their woefully inadequate school.

▲
A young African American drinks from a "colored" water fountain at the county courthouse in Halifax, North Carolina.

◄ Waiting for a bus in the segregated city of Memphis, Tennessee.

Protesting Integration Whites protest the integration of Calvary Church. ▶

Protesting School Segregation A protest march in St. Louis, Missouri.
▼

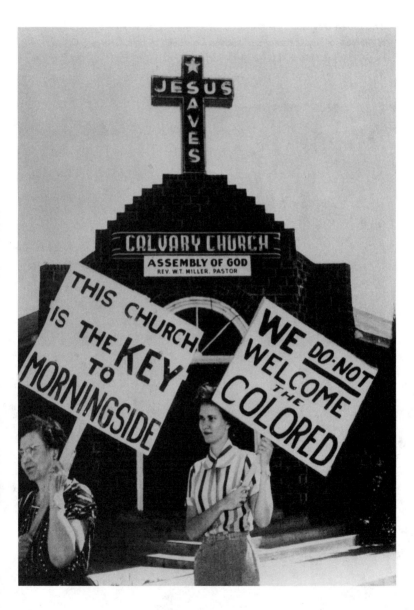

The *Brown* Decision The NAACP lawyers who argued *Brown v. Board of Education of Topeka* before the Supreme Court (left to right: George E. C. Hayes, Thurgood Marshall, James M. Nabrit).
▼

Marching Thurgood Marshall leading a protest march.
▼

The Protests Begin

The Montgomery Bus Boycott

RECOLLECTIONS OF ROSA PARKS AND YANCEY MARTIN

In the segregated South, African Americans rode in the back of the buses and were also expected to give up their seats if there were not enough seats for white passengers. On December 1, 1955, in Montgomery, Alabama, Rosa Parks was arrested when she refused to give up her seat. The African-American community of Montgomery rallied to support her. It was decided that African Americans would boycott the Montgomery bus system, and for more than a year this is what they did. Under the inspired leadership of a young minister named Martin Luther King, Jr., Montgomery's African-American citizens carpooled and walked to fight for their rights. Finally, the Supreme Court ruled that the laws that segregated Montgomery's buses were unconstitutional. In the following selections, Rosa Parks tells her own story and a young African American describes how everyone pitched in to keep the boycott going.

Rosa L. Parks

I had had problems with bus drivers over the years, because I didn't see fit to pay my money into the front and then go around to the back. Sometimes bus drivers wouldn't permit me to get on the bus, and I had been evicted from the bus. But as I say, there had been incidents over the years. One of the things that made this get so much publicity was the fact the police were called in and I was placed under arrest. See, if I had just been evicted from the bus and he hadn't placed me under arrest or had any charges brought against me, it probably could have been just another incident.

I had left my work at the men's alteration shop, a tailor shop in the Montgomery Fair department store, and as I left work, I crossed the street to a drugstore to pick up a few items instead of trying to go directly to the bus stop. And when I had finished this, I came across the street and looked for a Cleveland Avenue bus that apparently had some seats on it. At that time it was a little hard to get a seat on the bus. But when I did get to the entrance to the bus, I got in line with a number of other people who were getting on the same bus.

As I got up on the bus and walked to the seat I saw there was only one vacancy that was just back of where it was considered the white section. So this was the seat that I took, next to the aisle, and a man was sitting next to me. Across the aisle there were two women, and there were a few seats at this point in the very front of the bus that was called the white section. I went on to one stop and I didn't particularly notice who was getting on the bus, didn't particularly notice the other people getting on. And on the third stop there were some people getting on, and at this point all of the front seats were taken. Now in the beginning, at the very first stop I had got on the bus, the back of the bus was filled up with people standing in the aisle and I don't know why this one vacancy that I took was left, because there were quite a few people already standing toward the back of the bus. The third stop is when all the front seats were taken, and this one man was standing and when the driver looked around and saw he was standing, he asked the four of us, the man in the seat with me and the two women across the aisle, to let him have those front seats.

At his first request, didn't any of us move. Then he spoke again and said, "You'd better make it light on yourselves and let me have those seats." At this point, of course, the passenger who would have taken the seat hadn't said anything. In fact, he never did speak to my knowledge. When the three people, the man who was in the seat with me and the two women, stood up and moved into the aisle, I remained where I was. When the driver saw that I was still sitting there, he asked if I was going to stand up. I told him, no, I wasn't. He said, "Well, if you don't stand up, I'm going to have you arrested." I told him to go on and have me arrested.

He got off the bus and came back shortly. A few minutes later, two policemen got on the bus, and they approached me and asked if the driver had asked me to stand up, and I said yes, and they wanted to know why I didn't. I told them I didn't think I should have to stand up. After I had paid my fare and occupied a seat, I didn't think I should have to give it up. They placed me under arrest then and had me to get in the police car, and I was taken to jail and booked on suspicion, I believe. The questions were asked, the usual questions they ask a prisoner or somebody that's under arrest. They had to determine whether or not the driver wanted to press charges or swear out a warrant, which he did. Then they took me to jail and I was placed in a cell. In a little while I was taken from the cell, and my picture was made and fingerprints taken. I went back to the cell then, and a few minutes later I was called back again, and when this happened I found out that Mr. E. D. Nixon and Attorney and Mrs. Clifford Durr had come to make bond for me.

In the meantime before this, of course . . . I was given permission to make a telephone call after my picture was taken and fingerprints taken. I called my home and spoke to my mother on the telephone and told her what had happened, that I was in jail. She was quite upset and asked me had the police beaten me. I told her, no, I hadn't been physically injured, but I was being held in jail, and I wanted my husband to come and get me out. . . . He didn't have a car at that time, so he had to get someone to bring him down. At the time when he got down, Mr. Nixon and the Durrs had just made bond for me, so we all met at the jail and we went home. . . .

Yancey Martin

I came home from college in 1955 in December for Christmas holidays and the boycott had already begun when I got home. I don't remember the exact date that they started, but they were still in the churches and they were still having the meetings in the evening and they were still organizing it. . . .

I talked with an old friend of the family, Ralph Abernathy, who I had been in a play with while Ralph was in college with my brother. We were in a play called *On Whitman Avenue* and I played his grandson. And so I talked with him about what we could do, and he told me the best thing I could do was organize some people to do some driving along the bus stop route and to pick up people. 'Cause what they were doing was they were telling folk just to stand on their regular bus stop route, but as the bus would come by, just to step back. And so all the guys who were on my street . . . and a group of other folk whose parents had cars, we would all get up in the morning as early as we could. I mean, there were some folk out there who had to leave by six o'clock in order to get to the white lady's kitchen, and many times they were just late getting there. We'd all get up in the morning and we'd drive that route, like some would drive the South Jackson route, some would drive the Old Boston bus route, some would drive the Washington Park route, and we'd just mix it around . . . two or three cars per route 'cause you end up with a lot of people. And what we had to do was we had to know the names of everybody in there or else the police would stop and try to charge you with operating an illegal **jitney**[1] service. And so what we would do is, by knowing everybody's name, we'd just say that these are my cousins or these are friends of mine I'm giving a lift. There's no law against giving anybody a ride. But the police, when they found out what we were doing, they would patrol the bus routes just as much as we would.

After one of the mass meetings . . . I believe it was at Ralph's church, First Baptist Church, it was a decision made that people would not stand at the bus stop, would not get picked up at the bus stop, but either midway the block or just beyond the bus stop, so that police could not get you for picking people up at the bus stop. I don't know what kind of law that was, but for some reason or another that became a key issue as to where you picked people up and where you let them out. And then on Monroe Street just behind a building that was owned by a black doctor, . . . there was a parking lot for the patients he used to see and a taxi stand, black taxi stand. Well, that parking lot became a pick-up point.

But then what would happen . . . the tag numbers would be taken down by policemen, and then for other reasons you'd be harassed. Like, if you were out one night and you were at Gordon's Ice Cream Parlor, which was out on Hall Street, the police would see your car and know that you were one of the cars that were always involved in picking up the people. And then

---

[1] **jitney**—a small bus or van that transports passengers on a route for a small fare.

they'd just come in the place and ask who owned that car, and they'd say, "You're not parked close enough to the curb. . . ." They'd find something wrong to harass you about.

And what was really interesting was that the black folk knew that the movement did not have any money to pay for all this stuff. They were spending enough money on trying to get people out on bail bond if they got arrested. So people started giving you the nickel or the dime or whatever it was that they would give you for the bus, but not let nobody see it, so you could buy some gasoline. At that time, gas was nineteen cents a gallon or so, so you could just about get away without having to spend any of your own money on gasoline. Never asked anybody for anything, but they would just [say], "Here's a dime. . . . Here's a quarter I can give you to help you out with the gasoline." And I used to take that money and put it all back into the gas—well, almost all of it. I mighta saved a little bit of it out for a beer or something.

QUESTIONS TO CONSIDER

1. What is Rosa Parks's tone when she describes the incident on the bus?

2. What clues do you have that Parks was a courageous woman even before she was arrested for refusing to move to the back of the bus?

3. What role did Yancey Martin play in the bus boycott?

4. One woman who took part in the bus boycott was encouraged to get back on the bus because of her age. She refused, saying, "My feets is tired, but my soul is rested." In what way does her quote symbolize the entire Civil Rights movement?

Desegregating the Schools

Despite the Supreme Court's decision in Brown v. Board of Education of Topeka, *resistance to African-American students entering white schools was fierce and violent. The school district of Little Rock, Arkansas, drafted a plan for gradual integration, but when the first African-American students tried to attend classes at Central High School in 1957, Orval Faubus, the governor of Arkansas, sent out state troops to stop the integration. President Eisenhower ordered the National Guard to force the schools in Little Rock to obey the desegregation order. With military protection, nine students, the "Little Rock Nine," were eventually admitted. Elizabeth Eckford was one of those nine, and following are her recollections of the first day she tried to go to school.*

Federal troops were also required in 1963 to integrate the University of Mississippi. James Meredith, a veteran of the Korean War, enrolled at the University of Mississippi in Oxford. When the University tried to deny him entrance, federal court orders backed him up. Federal marshals protected Meredith as he registered.

Elizabeth Eckford, 16, Tries to Go to School

Before I left home Mother called us into the living-room. She said we should have a word of prayer. Then I caught the bus and got off a block from the school. I saw a large crowd of people standing across the street from the soldiers guarding Central. As I walked on, the crowd suddenly got very quiet. Superintendent Blossom had told us to enter by the front door. I looked at all the people and thought, "Maybe I will be safer if I walk down the block to the front entrance behind the guards."

At the corner I tried to pass through the long line of guards around the school so as to enter the grounds behind them. One of the guards pointed across the street. So I pointed in the same direction and asked whether he meant for me to cross the street and walk down. He nodded "yes." So, I walked across the street conscious of the crowd that stood there, but they moved away from me.

For a moment all I could hear was the shuffling of their feet. Then someone shouted, "Here she comes, get ready!" I moved away from the crowd on the sidewalk and into the street. If the mob came at me, I could then cross back over so the guards could protect me.

The crowd moved in closer and then began to follow me, calling me names. I still wasn't afraid. Just a little bit nervous. Then my knees started to shake all of a sudden and I wondered whether I could make it to the center entrance a block away. It was the longest block I ever walked in my whole life.

Even so, I still wasn't too scared because all the time I kept thinking that the guards would protect me.

When I got right in front of the school, I went up to a guard again. But this time he just looked straight ahead and didn't move to let me pass him. I didn't know what to do. Then I looked and saw that the path leading to the front entrance was a little further ahead. So I walked until I was right in front of the path to the front door.

I stood looking at the school—it looked so big! Just then the guards let some white students go through.

The crowd was quiet. I guess they were waiting to see what was going to happen. When I was able to steady my knees, I walked up to the guard who had let the white students in. He too didn't move. When I tried to squeeze past him, he raised his bayonet and then the other guards closed in and they raised their bayonets.

They glared at me with a mean look and I was very frightened and didn't know what to do. I turned around and the crowd came toward me.

They moved closer and closer. Somebody started yelling, "Lynch her! Lynch her!"

I tried to see a friendly face somewhere in the mob—someone who maybe would help. I looked into the face of an old woman and it seemed a kind face, but when I looked at her again, she spat on me.

They came closer, shouting, "No [racial epithet] is going to get in our school. Get out of here!"

I turned back to the guards but their faces told me I wouldn't get help from them. Then I looked down the block and saw a bench at the bus stop. I thought, "If I can only get there I will be safe." I don't know why the bench seemed a safe place to me, but I started walking toward it. I tried to close my mind to what they were shouting, and kept saying to myself, "If I can only make it to the bench I will be safe."

When I finally got there, I don't think I could have gone another step. I sat down and the mob crowded up and began shouting all over again. Someone hollered, "Drag her over to this tree! Let's take care of the [racial epithet]." Just then a white man sat down beside me, put his arm around me and patted my shoulder. He raised my chin and said, "Don't let them see you cry."

Then, a white lady—she was very nice—she came over to me on the bench. She spoke to me but I don't remember now what she said. She put me on the bus and sat next to me. She asked me my name and tried to talk to me but I don't think I answered. I can't remember much about the bus ride, but the next thing I remember I was standing in front of the School for the Blind, where Mother works.

I thought, "Maybe she isn't here. But she has to be here!" So I ran upstairs, and I think some teachers tried to talk to me, but I kept running until I reached Mother's classroom.

Mother was standing at the window with her head bowed, but she must have sensed I was there because she turned around. She looked as if she had been crying, and I wanted to tell her I was all right. But I couldn't speak. She put her arms around me and I cried.

James Meredith's Statement

In this time of crisis, I feel it appropriate for me to clarify my position as to my intention, my objectives, my hopes, and my desires.

For several months I have been involved in a struggle to gain admission to the University of Mississippi. The prime objective is, of course, to receive the educational training necessary to enable me to be a useful citizen of my own home state of Mississippi.

There are those in my state who oppose me in my efforts to obtain an education in the schools of my state. They do this because I am a Negro, and Negroes are not allowed to attend certain schools in my state. The schools that we are forbidden to attend are the only ones in the state that offer the training which I wish to receive. Consequently, those who oppose me are saying to me, we have given you what we want you to have and you can have no more. And if you want more than we have given you, then go to some other state or some other country and get your training.

What logic is it that concludes that a citizen of one state must be required to go to another state to receive the educational training that is normally and ordinarily offered and received by other citizens of that state? Further, what justification can there possibly be for one state to accept the responsibility for educating the citizens of another state when the training is offered to other citizens in the home state?

We have a dilemma. It is a fact that the Negroes of Mississippi are effectively not first-class citizens. I feel that every citizen should be a first-class citizen and should be allowed to develop his talents on a free, equal, and competitive basis. I think this is fair and that it infringes on the rights and privileges of no one. Certainly to be denied this opportunity is a violation of my rights as a citizen of the United States and the state of Mississippi.

The future of the United States of America, the future of the South, the future of Mississippi, and the future of the Negro rests on the decision of whether or not the Negro citizen is to be allowed to receive an education in his own state. If a state is permitted to **arbitrarily**[1] deny any right that is so basic to the American way of life to any citizen, then democracy is a failure.

I dream of the day when Negroes in Mississippi can live in decency and respect and do so without fear of intimidation and bodily harm or of receiving personal embarrassment, and with an assurance of equal justice under the law.

The price of progress is indeed high, but the price of holding it back is much higher.

---

[1] **arbitrarily**—based on individual preference and random choices rather than on fixed laws.

QUESTIONS TO CONSIDER

1. In the first selection, what motivates the guards and bystanders to act as they do toward Elizabeth Eckford?

2. Why does James Meredith object to being sent out of state for school?

3. In what way does Meredith believe that democracy is a failure in the United States?

from

Coming of Age in Mississippi

BY ANNE MOODY

On February 1, 1960, four African-American students from North Carolina Agricultural and Technical College walked into a store in Greensboro, North Carolina, and sat down at the lunch counter. The four young men held their seats until the lunch counter closed. The sit-in as a form of nonviolent protest was born. African Americans began staging sit-ins at lunch counters through-out Greensboro. After six months of nonviolent protest, Greensboro city officials were forced to relent and allow African Americans to be served at restaurants. In the spring of 1960, sit-in leaders from all over the South met in Raleigh, North Carolina, and founded the Student Nonviolent Coordinating Committee (SNCC, pronounced "snick"). The following selection is an excerpt from Anne Moody's autobiography Coming of Age in Mississippi *in which she describes a sit-in in Memphis.*

To divert attention from the sit-in at Woolworth's, the picketing started at J. C. Penney's a good fifteen minutes before. The pickets were allowed to walk up and down in front of the store three or four times before they were arrested. At exactly 11 A.M., Pearlena, Memphis, and I entered Woolworth's from the rear entrance. We separated as soon as we stepped into the store, and made small purchases from various counters. Pearlena had given Memphis her watch. He was to let us know when it was 11:14. At 11:14 we were to join him near the lunch counter and at exactly 11:15 we were to take seats at it.

Seconds before 11:15 we were occupying three seats at the previously segregated Woolworth's lunch counter. In the beginning the waitresses seemed to ignore us, as if they really didn't know what was going on. Our waitress walked past us a couple of times before she noticed we had started to write our own orders down and realized we wanted service. She asked us what we wanted. We began to read to her from our order slips. She told us that we would be served at the back counter, which was for Negroes.

"We would like to be served here," I said.

The waitress started to repeat what she had said, then stopped in the middle of the sentence. She turned the lights out behind the counter, and she and the other waitresses almost ran to the back of the store, deserting all their white customers. I guess they thought that violence would start immediately after the whites at the counter realized what was going on. There were five or six other people at the counter. A couple of them just got up and walked away. A girl sitting next to me finished her banana split before leaving. A middle-aged white woman who had not yet been served rose from her seat and came over to us. "I'd like to stay here with you," she said, "but my husband is waiting."

The newsmen came in just as she was leaving. They must have discovered what was going on shortly after some of the people began to leave the store. One of the newsmen ran behind the woman who spoke to us and asked her to identify herself. She refused to give her name, but said she was a native of Vicksburg and a former resident of California. When asked why she had said what she had said to us, she replied, "I am in sympathy with the Negro movement." By this time a crowd of cameramen and reporters had gathered around us taking pictures and asking questions, such as Where were we from? Why did we sit-in? What organization sponsored it? Were we students? From what school? How were we classified?

I told them that we were all students at Tougaloo College, that we were represented by no particular organization, and that we planned to stay there even after the store closed. "All we want is service," was my reply to one of them. After they had finished probing for about twenty minutes, they were almost ready to leave.

At noon, students from a nearby white high school started pouring in to Woolworth's. When they first saw us they were sort of surprised. They didn't know how to react. A few started to **heckle**[1] and the newsmen became interested again. Then the white students started chanting all kinds of anti-Negro slogans. We were called a little bit of everything. The rest of the seats except the three we were occupying had been roped off to prevent others from sitting down. A couple of the boys took one end of the rope and made it into a hangman's noose. Several attempts were made to put it around our necks. The crowds grew as more students and adults came in for lunch.

We kept our eyes straight forward and did not look at the crowd except for occasional glances to see what was going on. All of a sudden I saw a face I remembered— the drunkard from the bus station sit-in. My eyes

---

[1] **heckle**—harass.

lingered on him just long enough for us to recognize each other. Today he was drunk too, so I don't think he remembered where he had seen me before. He took out a knife, opened it, put it in his pocket, and then began to pace the floor. At this point, I told Memphis and Pearlena what was going on. Memphis suggested that we pray. We bowed our heads, and all hell broke loose. A man rushed forward, threw Memphis from his seat, and slapped my face. Then another man who worked in the store threw me against an adjoining counter.

Down on my knees on the floor, I saw Memphis lying near the lunch counter with blood running out of the corners of his mouth. As he tried to protect his face, the man who'd thrown him down kept kicking him against the head. If he had worn hard-soled shoes instead of sneakers, the first kick probably would have killed Memphis. Finally a man dressed in plain clothes identified himself as a police officer and arrested Memphis and his attacker.

Pearlena had been thrown to the floor. She and I got back on our stools after Memphis was arrested. There were some white Tougaloo teachers in the crowd. They asked Pearlena and me if we wanted to leave. They said that things were getting too rough. We didn't know what to do. While we were trying to make up our minds, we were joined by Joan Trumpauer. Now there were three of us and we were integrated. The crowd began to chant, "Communists, Communists, Communists." Some old man in the crowd ordered the students to take us off the stools.

"Which one should I get first?" a big husky boy said.

"That white [racial epithet]," the old man said.

The boy lifted Joan from the counter by her waist and carried her out of the store. Simultaneously, I was snatched from my stool by two high school students. I was dragged about thirty feet toward the door by my hair when someone made them turn me loose. As I was getting up off the floor, I saw Joan coming back inside. We started back to the center of the counter to join Pearlena. Lois Chaffee, a white Tougaloo faculty member, was now sitting next to her. So Joan and I just climbed across the rope at the front end of the counter and sat down. There were now four of us, two whites and two Negroes, all women. The mob started smearing us with ketchup, mustard, sugar, pies, and everything on the counter. Soon Joan and I were joined by John Salter, but the moment he sat down he was hit on the jaw with what appeared to be brass knuckles. Blood gushed from his face and someone threw salt into the open wound. Ed King, Tougaloo's chaplain, rushed to him.

At the other end of the counter, Lois and Pearlena were joined by George Raymond, a CORE field worker and a student from Jackson State College. Then a Negro high school boy sat down next to me. The mob took spray paint from the counter and sprayed it on the new demonstrators. The high school student had on a white shirt; the word "[racial epithet]" was written on his back with red spray paint.

We sat there for three hours taking a beating when the manager decided to close the store because the mob had begun to go wild with stuff from other counters. He begged and begged everyone to leave.

But even after fifteen minutes of begging, no one budged. They would not leave until we did. Then Dr. Beittel, the president of Tougaloo College, came running in. He said he had just heard what was happening.

About ninety policemen were standing outside the store; they had been watching the whole thing through the windows, but had not come in to stop the mob or do anything. President Beittel went outside and asked Captain Ray to come and escort us out. The captain refused, stating the manager had to invite him in before he could enter the premises, so Dr. Beittel himself brought us out. He had told the police that they had better protect us after we were outside the store. When we got outside, the policemen formed a single line that blocked the mob from us. However, they were allowed to throw at us everything they had collected. Within ten minutes, we were picked up by Reverend King in his station wagon and taken to the NAACP headquarters on Lynch Street.

After the sit-in, all I could think of was how sick Mississippi whites were. They believed so much in the segregated Southern way of life, they would kill to preserve it. I sat there in the NAACP office and thought of how many times they had killed when this way of life was threatened. I knew that the killing had just begun. "Many more will die before it is over with," I thought. Before the sit-in, I had always hated the whites in Mississippi. Now I knew it was impossible for me to hate sickness. The whites had a disease, an incurable disease in its final stage. What were our chances against such a disease? I thought of the students, the young Negroes who had just begun to protest, as young interns. When these young interns got older, I thought, they would be the best doctors in the world for social problems.

QUESTIONS TO CONSIDER

1. What was the purpose of the sit-in at Woolworth's?

2. Why did the three students—Anne, Pearlena, and Memphis—continue to sit quietly at the counter despite everything that was going on around them?

3. Why do you think the white Southerners were so threatened by the prospect of desegregation?

from

Revolution in Mississippi *and* Letter from a Mississippi Jail Cell

Following on the heels of the successful sit-ins of 1960, SNCC (Student Nonviolent Coordinating Committee) organized a voter registration campaign. One of the heads of this campaign was Robert Moses, a Harvard-educated teacher who had given up his job in New York to take part in the fight for rights. During the campaign, Moses and his fellow workers were regularly beaten and imprisoned. Tom Hayden was a student who spent a summer in Mississippi reporting on the Civil Rights movement. His report Revolution in Mississippi *describes the voter registration campaign and the reaction of whites. After his experiences in the South, Hayden gave up journalism and went on to become one of the most famous activists in America, leading the Students for a Democratic Society to national prominence. Below is an excerpt from Hayden's report and a letter written by Moses while languishing in a Mississippi jail.*

from *Revolution in Mississippi*
by Tom Hayden

SNCC, in its attempt to ignite a mass non-violent movement, designated the formidable and sovereign state of Mississippi as the site of its pilot project. [Robert] Moses moved to McComb, a city of 13,000. He found a number of local adults, high school students, and non-student youth eager to assist him. They provided contacts, housing, some transportation and (particularly the students) began canvassing the surrounding area, determining the numbers of registered and unregistered voters, informing the citizens of the SNCC program and inviting them to participate. By the end of the first week, John Hardy, Nashville, and Reggie Robinson, Baltimore, had arrived as SNCC field representatives to help in the project.

On August 7, 1961, the SNCC Voter Registration School opened in Burglundtown in a combination cinder block-and-paintless wood frame two-story structure which houses a grocery below and a Masonic meeting hall above. A typical voter registration (or citizenship) class involved a study of the Mississippi State Constitution, filling out of sample application forms, description of the typical habits of the Southern registrar —whose **discretionary**[1] powers are enormous—and primarily attempted the morale building, encouragement and consequent group identification which might inspire the exploited to attempt registration.

On the first day of the school, four persons went down to the registrar's office in nearby Magnolia, the county seat of Pike; three of them registered successfully. Three went down on August 9th; two were registered. Nine went down on August 10th; one was registered. By this time, articles in the local press, the (McComb)

---

[1] **discretionary**—involving individual choice or judgment.

Enterprise-Journal, had increased awareness of the project, stirring a few Negroes from Walthall and Amite to come to the McComb classes. However, the thrust of the movement was somewhat blunted on the evening of August 10th when one of the Negroes who had attempted to register was shot at by a white. (It is now clear that the shooting had nothing to do with the attempted registration that day. However, in the minds of the Negro community, for whom the vote is intimately connected with intimidation and violence, the association was made between the two events.) Attendance at the Voter Registration School quickly diminished. . . .

On August 18th, Marion Barry from Nashville, a SNCC field representative particularly concerned with initiating direct action, arrived in McComb. Those students too young to vote, many of whom had canvassed regularly, were eager to participate actively. The Pike County Non-Violent Movement was formed; workshops in the theory and practice of non-violence were held. On August 26th two of the youths, Elmer Hayes and Hollis Watkins (both 18), sat-in at the lunch counter of the local Woolworth's, the first direct action incident in the history of the county. The two were arrested and remained in jail 30 days. The charge: breach of peace. Their arrest set the stage for a mass meeting in McComb on August 29th. The Reverend James Bevel, of Jackson, spoke to a crowd of nearly 200. The paper of the following day carried the story lead, in large type, and the local columnists warned the citizens that the Negroes were not engaged in a mere passing fad, but were serious in intention.

On August 30th, a sit-in occurred at the lunch counter of the local bus station. Isaac Lewis, 20, Robert Talbert, 19, and Brenda Lewis, 16, were arrested on charges of breach of peace and failure to move on. They remained in jail for 28 days. By now, a current of protest had been generated throughout the counties.

Subsequent events intensified the feeling. On August 29th, Bob Moses took two persons to the registrar's office in Liberty. They were met by Billy Jack Caston, (cousin of the sheriff and son-in-law of State Representative Eugene Hurst) who was accompanied by another cousin and the son of the sheriff. (Should this seem peculiar, read Faulkner.) Caston smashed Moses across the head and dropped him to the street. The other Negroes were not harmed. Moses' cuts required eight stitches. Moses filed assault and battery charges against Caston, perhaps the first time in the history of Amite that a Negro has legally contested the right of a white man to mutilate him at fancy. Approximately 150 whites attended the trial on August 31st. Among other questions, Caston's attorney asked Moses if he had participated in the riots in San Francisco or Japan; Moses replied that he had not. Upon the suggestion of law officials, Moses left the trial, at which he was the plaintiff, before the "not guilty" verdict in order to escape mass assault. . . .

The students—remember, 100 under 18 years of age—spent the mid-day preparing signs, and at about 2:30 P.M., they started to march downtown. Never before in McComb—never before in an area so rural, so violent—never before anywhere in the South with students so very young. One of them, 13 years old, has been charged with "assault with intent to kill" because she ran over the foot of a white woman in a supermarket with a push-cart, and, subsequently, the two slapped each other. That is simply an example. The others, while a little older, suffer the same system and are moved by the same courage. And so they went downtown—with 119 in all, including 19 students over age 18, Bob Moses, Charles McDew and Robert Zellner. They walked through the Negro neighborhoods where families watched from the windows and steps and yards, through the downtown business district, down to the edge of McComb, and back up to City Hall. There the march halted. Elmer Hayes, one of the original McComb sit-inners, began to pray on the steps. Three times the police asked him to move on. He refused and was arrested. Then it was Lewis, Talbert, and the 16-year-old Brenda, in order, all arrested, Brenda violating juvenile parole. Each individual in the march stood quietly, waiting to be arrested. Moments before, a white man had tried to run over them with his automobile; now there were whites on foot, yelling, cursing. And each of the 114 left was quietly standing. Too much time was being taken up, so the police blew their whistles and pronounced everyone under arrest.

The whole march started up the stairs, on its way to be booked. As they did, a local white citizen reached out for Zellner and began to beat him. Hurting Zellner with the first punch, the man then grabbed him around the neck and began choking him and gouging his eyes. Then Bob Moses and Charles McDew were there, one holding the white's wrists, one clasping Zellner in protection. Moses and McDew were struck and dragged into the station by police, who then pulled in Zellner. The first statement inside the Police Chief's office, according to Zellner, was, "Ought to leave you out there." Everyone was arrested and placed in jail.

Letter from a Mississippi Jail Cell
by Robert Moses

We are smuggling this note from the drunk tank of the county jail in Magnolia, Mississippi. Twelve of us are here, sprawled out along the concrete bunker; Curtis Hayes, Hollis Watkins, Ike Lewis and Robert Talbert, four veterans of the bunker, are sitting up talking —mostly about girls; Charles McDew ("Tell the story") is curled into the concrete and the wall; Harold Robinson, Stephen Ashley, James Wells, Lee Chester, Vick, Leotus Eubanks, and Ivory Diggs lay cramped on the cold bunker; I'm sitting with smuggled pen and paper, thinking a little, writing a little; Myrtis Bennett and Janie Campbell are across the way wedded to a different icy cubicle.

Later on Hollis will lead out with a clear tenor into a freedom song; Talbert and Lewis will supply jokes; and McDew will discourse on the history of the black man and the Jew. McDew—a black by birth, a Jew by choice and a revolutionary by necessity—has taken on the deep hates and deep loves which America, and the world, reserve for those who dare to stand in a strong sun and cast a sharp shadow.

In the words of Judge Brumfield, who sentenced us, we are "cold calculators" who design to disrupt the racial harmony (harmonious since 1619) of McComb into racial strife and rioting; we, he said, are the leaders who are causing young children to be led like sheep to the pen to be slaughtered (in a legal manner). "Robert," he was addressing me, "haven't some of the people from your school been able to go down and register without violence here in Pike county?" I thought to myself that Southerners are most exposed when they boast.

It's mealtime now: we have rice and gravy in a flat pan, dry bread and a "big town cake"; we lack eating and drinking utensils. Water comes from a faucet and goes into a hole.

This is Mississippi, the middle of the iceberg. Hollis is leading off with his tenor, "Michael, row the boat ashore, Alleluia; Christian brothers don't be slow, Alleluia; Mississippi's next to go, Alleluia." This is a tremor in the middle of the iceberg—from a stone that the builders rejected.

QUESTIONS TO CONSIDER

1. After the 114 protesters are taken into custody, the police chief says, "Ought to leave you out there." What does his statement reveal about his attitude?

2. Does Robert Moses regret the actions that led to his being thrown in jail? Explain your opinion.

3. If Mississippi is the iceberg, then what is the "tremor"? Who has thrown the stone that caused this tremor?

The Protest Begins

Montgomery Bus Boycott Rosa Parks being fingerprinted after she was arrested for refusing to give up her seat on a bus.

▲
Meeting at the Mt. Zion Church Martin Luther King, Jr., preaching to supporters in Montgomery, Alabama. King led the bus boycott after Mrs. Parks's arrest.

If They Stay, We Go White students protesting integration in Little Rock schools. ▶

Integrating the Schools Mississippi national guardsmen escort African-American students attending a formerly all-white school in Mississippi.

▼

Marching The NAACP and other groups march to protest segregated schools.

▲
Federal marshals protect James Meredith as he prepares to register at the University of Mississippi.

The Movement Spreads

from

Freedom Ride

BY JAMES PECK

*In May 1961, a group of black and white men and women set out
from Washington, D.C., in two buses. Calling themselves "Freedom
Riders," they wanted to force the integration of bus terminals
throughout the South. In Anniston, Alabama, a mob attacked the
buses, destroying one and beating the riders. They were attacked
again in Birmingham and Montgomery, leading the federal government to send federal marshals to protect the riders. The escalating
violence led the government to put pressure on the Interstate
Commerce Commission to end segregation in public transport facilities
later that summer. James Peck was one of the first sixteen
Freedom Riders. In an excerpt from his book* Freedom Ride, *he
describes the stages of the ride and the violence in Birmingham.*

Charlotte was the scene of the trip's first arrest—
and the birth of a new "in," the shoe-in. Charles Person
climbed onto a shoeshine chair and, after being refused
service, remained seated until a cop with handcuffs
arrived. Person then left, since no policy regarding

shoeshines had yet been decided by the group and, as on the Journey, each step and who was to take it would be decided at group meetings before every lap of the Ride. When Person went for the shine, he didn't even think of it as a test. He simply looked at his shoes and thought he needed a shine. It was then hastily decided by the group that Joe Perkins should make a test and stay in the shoeshine chair until arrested. The trip's first arrest came within minutes. Attorney Thomas Wyche won an acquittal on the basis of the Supreme Court's *Boynton* decision, and Perkins rejoined us a day later.

Violence against the Freedom Riders erupted for the first time in Rock Hill, South Carolina, where the press had headlined our arrival and where hoodlums had recently attacked lunch-counter pickets. In fact several of the hoodlums waiting at the Greyhound station were recognized as the same individuals who had assaulted the local student pickets.

As the Greyhound contingent of Riders arrived, some twenty of these ruffians were waiting. When John Lewis, who is Negro, approached the entrance of the white waiting room, he was assaulted by two of them. Three started slugging Albert Bigelow, a white, who was next in line.

Aside from their commitment to nonviolence, these two Freedom Riders were as dissimilar as any two individuals could possibly be. Lewis is a short, muscular divinity student. Bigelow is a tall, grey-haired, ex-naval commander. Lewis is **taciturn**.[1] Bigelow is articulate. Lewis is one of ten children born on a southern Alabama farm—the only one to finish high school. Bigelow's family background is blueblood,[2] New England. Lewis got his extensive nonviolent training during the lunch counter sit-ins in Nashville, where he was studying for

---

[1] **taciturn**—habitually untalkative.

[2] blueblood—one who is a member of a socially prominent family.

the ministry. Bigelow became a pacifist in revulsion over his World War II experiences as a naval commander and had, like me, participated in protest actions against nuclear tests and war. Had it not been for the Freedom Rides, these two never would have met. Yet, here they were together, being slugged in front of the Greyhound terminal in Rock Hill, South Carolina, and remaining completely nonviolent.

In the course of the slugging, Genevieve Hughes, who was behind Lewis and Bigelow, was pushed to the ground. At that point the police, who had been standing by but taking time in performance of their duty, arrived. The police captain asked Lewis and Bigelow whether they wanted to press charges against any of their assailants. They declined. Thereupon, the Riders entered the white waiting room unmolested.

When the group with which I was riding arrived at the Trailways terminal a few hours later, some of the hoodlums were waiting in cars. However, they did not attack, but only drove after us a few blocks toward Friendship Junior College. The Trailways terminal building was completely locked up. Its eating facilities had been closed since Friendship students had conducted sit-ins there. . . .

At Sumter, both on arrival and on departure, the white waiting room was tested without incident. There is no restaurant in the Sumter terminal.

In Augusta, Georgia, at both the Trailways and Greyhound terminals, Freedom Riders used all facilities without incident. It marked the first time that Negroes had ever eaten at the terminal restaurants. In fact, only a few months before, a Negro serviceman had been arrested for trying to eat there. Yet our presence at the tables drew little attention. Neither racist hoodlums nor mere curiosity seekers gathered.

To make sure that the policy change was not solely for our arrival and departure, a test team—Herman Harris and Walter Bergman—went back to both terminal restaurants during the evening of our overnight stop and were served courteously.

The rest stop on the way from Augusta to Atlanta was Athens, scene, the previous fall, of mob action against admission of two Negro students to college. Freedom Riders were served at the lunch counter without question. Again, there were no gapers. A person viewing the Athens desegregated lunch counter and waiting room during our fifteen-minute rest stop might have imagined himself at a rest stop up North rather than deep in Georgia.

In Atlanta we were welcomed at the Greyhound terminal by a large group of students, many of whom had participated in the local lunch-counter picketing and sit-ins. The terminal restaurant was closed but we used the waiting room and rest rooms. The Trailways terminal restaurant was open and two of our teams tested it on departure without incident. During our evening in Atlanta, Martin Luther King, who lives there, stopped by to talk with us and express his support. So did Lonnie King and Ed King, local student leaders. (Neither is related to Martin Luther King.)

Our experiences in traveling through Georgia were clear proof of how desegregation can come peacefully in a Deep South state, providing there is no deliberate **incitement**[3] to hatred and violence by local or state political leaders. In Alabama, it was the flagrant incitement on the part of Governor Patterson, Eugene "Bull" Connor, Birmingham's notorious police chief, and other high-placed politicians which built up the mob violence which we were to face.

---

[3] **incitement**—a stirring up and urging on.

The most nightmarish day of our Freedom Ride was Sunday, May 14, Mother's Day. I identify the date with Mother's Day because when Police Chief Connor was asked why there was not a single policeman at the Birmingham Trailways terminal to avert mob violence, he explained that since it was Mother's Day, most of the police were off duty visiting their mothers. That there was going to be a mob to meet us had been well known around Birmingham for several days. Reverend Fred Shuttlesworth told me so when I phoned to give him the scheduled arrival times of our two buses.

However, we did not know in advance that a similar mob was waiting in Anniston, a rest stop on the way. Our first contingent, aboard Greyhound, learned of this when their bus stopped just outside of Anniston and their driver conferred briefly with the driver of a bus going the other way.

When the Greyhound bus pulled into Anniston, it was immediately surrounded by an angry mob armed with iron bars. They set upon the vehicle, denting the sides, breaking windows, and slashing tires. Finally, police arrived and the bus managed to depart. But the mob pursued it in cars. One car got ahead of the bus and prevented it from gathering speed. About six miles out, one of the tires went flat and the bus was forced to pull over to a gas station.

Within minutes, the pursuing mob was again hitting the bus with iron bars. The rear window was broken and a bomb was hurled inside. Suddenly the vehicle became filled with thick smoke. The passengers, including the Freedom Riders, ducked toward the floor in order to breathe. A few climbed out of a window. Some tried to get out the door, but it was being held shut from the outside.

As Henry Thomas tells it, he shortly succeeded in pushing the door open. As he stepped out, he walked toward a man who looked friendly. Suddenly the man wielded a club from behind his back and struck him over the head.

All the passengers managed to escape before the bus burst into flames and was totally destroyed. The extent of the destruction was shown in the grim newspaper photos of its charred interior and exterior. Policemen, who had been standing by, belatedly came on the scene. A couple of them fired shots in the air. The mob dispersed and the injured were taken to a local hospital. The Freedom Riders were finally transported to Birmingham in cars dispatched by Reverend Shuttlesworth.

When the Trailways bus carrying our contingent arrived in Anniston an hour later, the other passengers learned of what had happened to the Greyhound bus and discontinued their trip. While waiting for the bus to proceed, we heard the sirens of ambulances taking the injured to the hospital, but we didn't know what had happened.

We learned of it only when eight hoodlums climbed aboard and stood by the driver as he made a brief announcement. He concluded by stating that he would refuse to drive on unless the Negroes in our group moved to the formerly segregated rear seats. They remained quietly in their front seats. The hoodlums cursed and started to move them bodily to the rear, kicking and hitting them at the same time.

Walter Bergman, who is a retired professor, and I were seated toward the rear. We moved forward and tried to persuade the hoodlums to desist. We, too, were pushed, punched, and kicked. I found myself face downward on the floor of the bus. Someone was on top of me. I was bleeding. Bergman's jaw was cut and swollen. None of us realized that he also had received a crushing blow on the head which would bring him close to death four months later. Following an appendicitis operation, he suffered an almost fatal stroke which attending doctors attributed to a "pre-existent condition of brain damage" resulting from the Anniston assault. They notified police, because had Bergman died, it would have been a case of murder. Fortunately he recovered.

Mrs. Bergman, who observed the beating, commented later, "I had never before heard the sound of human flesh being hit; it was terrible!"

Finally, all of our group—whites and Negroes—and one Negro passenger who had not gotten off, had been forced to the back of the bus. The hoodlums—together with a pregnant woman whom they had brought aboard—sat in the very front. The seats in between remained empty. At that point the driver agreed to proceed to Birmingham. Some of us doubted whether he would really head there or turn up some obscure side road for another mob scene. For the entire two-hour ride to Birmingham, the hoodlums craned their necks to make sure we didn't move into any of the empty rows of front seats.

Upon arrival in Birmingham, I could see a mob lined up on the sidewalk only a few feet from the loading platform. Most of them were young—in their twenties. Some were carrying ill-concealed iron bars. A few were older men. All had hate showing on their faces.

I looked at them and then I looked at Charles Person, who had been designated as my team mate to test the lunch counter. Person, a slim youth, quiet and determined, had been jailed-in for sixteen days during the campaign to desegregate Atlanta lunch counters. On our overnight stop in Atlanta he visited his parents— reluctantly, he said, because he knew they would try to dissuade him from continuing the Freedom Ride. At departure time, one of us wondered whether the parents had prevailed. Most of us were confident that they hadn't and sure enough, just as we were leaving for the bus station, Person appeared.

Now we stood on the Birmingham unloading platform with the segregationist mob only a few feet away. I did not want to put Person in a position of being forced to proceed if he thought the situation too dangerous. When I looked at him, he responded by saying simply, "Let's go."

As we entered the white waiting room and approached the lunch counter, we were grabbed bodily and pushed toward the alleyway leading to the loading platform. As soon as we got into the alleyway and out of sight of onlookers in the waiting room, six of them started swinging at me with fists and pipes. Five others attacked Person a few feet ahead. Within seconds, I was unconscious on the ground.

I learned only later that the mob went on to assault Tom Langston of the Birmingham *Post-Herald* and smashed his camera. Langston had been sufficiently quick-witted to remove his film, and the photo of my beating, clearly showing the hate-filled expression of my assailants, appeared in next morning's *Post-Herald* and in many newspapers throughout the country. Then, Clancy Lake, a radio newsman, was attacked as he sat in his car, broadcasting an account of the onslaught.

When I regained consciousness, the alleyway was empty. Blood was flowing down my face. I tried to stop the flow with a handkerchief but it soon became soaked. A white soldier came out of the waiting room to see whether I needed help. I declined, because I suddenly saw Bergman coming from the loading platform. He helped me to get a cab. The first two refused to take me, but a third agreed. I told the driver to go to the home of Reverend Shuttlesworth, which was our Birmingham headquarters.

The first thing Reverend Shuttlesworth said to me as I got out of the cab was, "You need to go to a hospital." He called an ambulance. While waiting for it to arrive,

I looked for Person among the assembled Negro onlookers. I finally found him and we shook hands. He had a gash in the back of his head and his face was swollen, but he did not require hospitalization. I did not realize how seriously I had been hurt. My head required fifty-three stitches. X rays were taken to determine whether my skull had been fractured and whether my ribs were intact.

QUESTIONS TO CONSIDER

1. What do such terms as "Journey" and "Freedom Rider" remind you of? What effect do these words have?

2. Do you think the Freedom Riders considered this leg of their trip—from South Carolina and Georgia and into Alabama—a success? Why or why not?

3. What do you think gives these young men and women the courage to continue their struggle, even in the face of so much violence and hatred?

Protest Songs

The singing of folk songs and hymns was a way for Civil Rights protesters to express their beliefs and unity. The songs were sung at marches, sit-ins, on the Freedom Rides, and everywhere that African Americans were banding together to fight for their rights. Old songs took on new meanings during this struggle. The folk singer Pete Seeger said the protesters were "putting new words into the old songs, including a lot of friends and foes in the integration battle. To hear them singing these songs with hands clapping and bodies swaying and faces lighted up with a fierce joy of the freedom struggle was an experience I'll never forget." Following are the lyrics to three of the most famous songs of the Civil Rights movement.

We Shall Overcome

We shall overcome,
We shall overcome,
We shall overcome some day.
Oh, deep in my heart
I do believe
We shall overcome some day.

We shall walk in peace,
We shall walk in peace,
We shall walk in peace some day.
Oh, deep in my heart
I do believe
We shall walk in peace some day.

We shall build a new world,
We shall build a new world,
We shall build a new world some day.
Oh, deep in my heart
I do believe
We shall build a new world some day.

Oh, Freedom

Oh, Freedom
Oh, Freedom!
Oh, Freedom!
Oh, Freedom over me!
And before I'd be a slave,
I'd be buried in my grave,
And go home to my Lord and be free!

No more mournin'
No more weepin'
No more misery over me!
And before I'd be a slave,
I'd be buried in my grave,
And go home to my Lord and be free.

Keep Your Eyes on the Prize

Paul and Silas, bound in jail,
Had no money for to go their bail.

Chorus:
Keep your eyes on the prize.
Hold on, hold on,
Hold on, hold on—
Keep your eyes on the prize,
Hold on, hold on.

Paul and Silas began to shout,
The jail door opened and they walked out.
Freedom's name is mighty sweet—
Soon one of these days we're going to meet.

Got my hand on the Gospel plow
I wouldn't take nothing for my journey now.

The only chain that a man can stand
Is that chain of hand in hand.

The only thing that we did wrong—
Stayed in the wilderness too long.

But the one thing we did right
Was the day we started to fight.

We're gonna board that big Greyhound
Carryin' love from town to town.

We're gonna ride for civil rights,
We're gonna ride, both black and white.

We've met jail and violence too,
But God's love has seen us through.

Haven't been to heaven but I've been told
Streets up there are paved with gold.

QUESTIONS TO CONSIDER

1. What is it that the singers of "We Shall Overcome" hope
   to overcome?

2. What is the "prize" in "Keep Your Eyes on the Prize"?

3. From these songs, how important do you think it is for
   those in the Movement to have faith in God and religion?

from

Letter from a Birmingham Jail

BY MARTIN LUTHER KING, JR.

Birmingham, Alabama, was as segregated as a city could get in 1963. The chief of police, Eugene "Bull" Connor, was bitterly opposed to the Civil Rights movement. Reverend Martin Luther King, Jr., announced that he would lead demonstrations in Birmingham until the city integrated. Nonviolent marches began in April. Day after day, marchers were arrested and jailed, and King himself was arrested on April 12.

On May 3, Connor unleashed police dogs and men with fire-hoses on a peaceful march. The violence of the police was broadcast throughout the United States, causing an uproar. Finally, the Birmingham Chamber of Commerce negotiated an agreement to end the protests: public facilities were integrated, it was agreed that firms would begin hiring African Americans, and all demonstrators were released from jail. Below is an excerpt from King's "Letter from a Birmingham Jail."

April 16, 1963

My Dear Fellow Clergymen:

While confined here in the Birmingham city jail, I came across your recent statement calling my present activities "unwise and untimely." Seldom do I pause to answer criticism of my work and ideas. If I sought to answer all the criticisms that cross my desk, my secretaries would have little time for anything other than such correspondence in the course of the day, and I would have no time for constructive work. But since I feel that you are men of genuine good will and that your criticisms are sincerely set forth, I want to try to answer your statement in what I hope will be patient and reasonable terms. . . .

In any nonviolent campaign there are four basic steps: collection of the facts to determine whether injustices exist; negotiation; self-purification; and direct action. We have gone through all these steps in Birmingham. There can be no gainsaying the fact that racial injustice engulfs this community. Birmingham is probably the most thoroughly segregated city in the United States. Its ugly record of brutality is widely known. Negroes have experienced grossly unjust treatment in the courts. There have been more unsolved bombings of Negro homes and churches in Birmingham than in any other city in the nation. These are the hard, brutal facts of the case. . . .

You may well ask: "Why direct action? Why sit-ins, marches and so forth? Isn't negotiation a better path?" You are quite right in calling for negotiation. Indeed, this is the very purpose of direct action. Nonviolent direct action seeks to create such a crisis and foster such a tension that a community which has constantly refused to negotiate is forced to confront the issue. It seeks so to dramatize the issue that it can no longer be ignored. My citing the creation of tension as part of the work of the nonviolent-resister may sound rather shocking. But I must confess that I am not afraid of the word "tension." I have earnestly opposed violent tension, but there is a type of constructive, nonviolent tension which is necessary for growth. Just as Socrates felt that it was necessary to create a tension in the mind so that individuals could rise from the bondage of myths and half-truths to the **unfettered**[1] realm of creative analysis and objective appraisal, so must we see the need for nonviolent gadflies to create the kind of tension in society that will help men rise from the dark depths of prejudice and racism to the majestic heights of understanding and brotherhood.

The purpose of our direct-action program is to create a situation so crisis-packed that it will inevitably open the door to negotiation. I therefore concur with you in your call for negotiation. Too long has our beloved Southland been bogged down in a tragic effort to live in monologue rather than dialogue. . . .

We know through painful experience that freedom is never voluntarily given by the oppressor; it must be demanded by the oppressed. Frankly, I have yet to engage in a direct-action campaign that was "well timed" in the view of those who have not suffered unduly from the disease of segregation. For years now I have heard the word "Wait!" It rings in the ear of every Negro with piercing familiarity. This "Wait" has almost always meant "Never." We must come to see, with one of our distinguished jurists, that "justice too long delayed is justice denied."

We have waited for more than 340 years for our constitutional and God-given rights. The nations of Asia and Africa are moving with jetlike speed toward

---

[1] **unfettered**—freed.

gaining political independence, but we still creep at horse-and-buggy pace toward gaining a cup of coffee at a lunch counter. Perhaps it is easy for those who have never felt the stinging darts of segregation to say, "Wait." But when you have seen vicious mobs lynch your mothers and fathers at will and drown your sisters and brothers at whim; when you have seen hate-filled policemen curse, kick and even kill your black brothers and sisters; when you see the vast majority of your twenty million Negro brothers smothering in an airtight cage of poverty in the midst of an affluent society; when you suddenly find your tongue twisted and your speech stammering as you seek to explain to your six-year-old daughter why she can't go to the public amusement park that has just been advertised on television, and see tears welling up in her eyes when she is told that Funtown is closed to colored children, and see ominous clouds of inferiority beginning to form in her little mental sky, and see her beginning to distort her personality by develop-ing an unconscious bitterness toward white people; when you have to concoct an answer for a five-year-old son who is asking: "Daddy, why do white people treat colored people so mean?"; when you take a cross-country drive and find it necessary to sleep night after night in the uncomfortable corners of your automobile because no motel will accept you; when you are humiliated day in and day out by nagging signs reading "white" and "colored"; when your first name becomes "[racial epi-thet]," your middle name becomes "boy" (however old you are) and your last name becomes "John," and your wife and mother are never given the respected title "Mrs."; when you are harried by day and haunted by night by the fact that you are a Negro, living constantly at tiptoe stance, never quite knowing what to expect next, and are plagued with inner fears and outer resent-ments; when you are forever fighting a degenerating sense of "nobodiness"—then you will understand why we find it difficult to wait. There comes a time when the cup of endurance runs over, and men are no longer willing to be plunged into the **abyss**[2] of despair. I hope, sirs, you can understand our legitimate and unavoidable impatience. . . .

I must make two honest confessions to you, my Christian and Jewish brothers. First, I must confess that over the past few years I have been gravely disappointed with the white **moderate**.[3] I have almost reached the regrettable conclusion that the Negro's great stumbling block in his stride toward freedom is not the White Citizen's Councilor or the Ku Klux Klanner, but the white moderate, who is more devoted to "order" than to justice; who prefers a negative peace which is the absence of tension to a positive peace which is the presence of justice; who constantly says: "I agree with you in the goal you seek, but I cannot agree with your methods of direct action"; who **paternalistically**[4] believes he can set the timetable for another man's freedom; who lives by a mythical concept of time and who constantly advises the Negro to wait for a "more convenient season." Shallow understanding from people of good will is more frustrating than absolute misunderstanding from people of ill will. Lukewarm acceptance is much more bewildering than outright rejection.

I had hoped that the white moderate would understand that law and order exist for the purpose of establishing justice and that when they fail in this purpose they become the dangerously structured dams that block the flow of social progress. I had hoped that the white moderate would understand that the present tension in the South is a necessary phase of the transition from an obnoxious negative peace, in which the Negro

---

[2] **abyss**—an unfathomable chasm; a yawning gulf.

[3] **moderate**—one who holds political and social views that avoid extremes.

[4] **paternalistically**—like a father who deals benevolently and often intrusively with his children.

passively accepted his unjust plight, to a substantive and positive peace, in which all men will respect the dignity and worth of human personality. Actually, we who engage in nonviolent direct action are not the creators of tension. We merely bring to the surface the hidden tension that is already alive. We bring it out in the open, where it can be seen and dealt with. Like a boil that can never be cured so long as it is covered up but must be opened with all its ugliness to the natural medicines of air and light, injustice must be exposed, with all the tension its exposure creates, to the light of human conscience and the air of national opinion before it can be cured.

In your statement you assert that our actions, even though peaceful, must be condemned because they precipitate violence. But is this a logical assertion? Isn't this like condemning a robbed man because his possession of money precipitated the evil act of robbery? Isn't this like condemning Socrates because his unswerving commitment to truth and his philosophical inquiries precipitated the act by the misguided populace in which they made him drink hemlock? Isn't this like condemning Jesus because his unique God-consciousness and never-ceasing devotion to God's will precipitated the evil act of crucifixion? We must come to see that, as the federal courts have consistently affirmed, it is wrong to urge an individual to cease his efforts to gain his basic constitutional rights because the quest may precipitate violence. Society must protect the robbed and punish the robber.

I had also hoped that the white moderate would reject the myth concerning time in relation to the struggle for freedom. I have just received a letter from a white brother in Texas. He writes: "All Christians know that the colored people will receive equal rights eventually, but it is possible that you are in too great a religious hurry. It has taken Christianity almost two thousand years to accomplish what it has. The teachings of Christ take time to come to earth." Such an attitude stems from a tragic misconception of time, from the strangely irrational notion that there is something in the very flow of time that will inevitably cure all ills. Actually, time itself is neutral; it can be used either destructively or constructively. More and more I feel that the people of ill will have used time much more effectively than have the people of good will. We will have to repent in this generation not merely for the hateful words and actions of the bad people but for the appalling silence of the good people. Human progress never rolls in on wheels of inevitability; it comes through the tireless efforts of men willing to be co-workers with God, and without this hard work, time itself becomes an ally of the forces of social stagnation. We must use time creatively, in the knowledge that the time is always ripe to do right. Now is the time to make real the promise of democracy and transform our pending national **elegy**[5] into a creative psalm of brotherhood. Now is the time to lift our national policy from the quicksand of racial injustice to the solid rock of human dignity.

---

[5] **elegy**—a poem or song of death and dying.

QUESTIONS TO CONSIDER

1. How does the creation of "tension" play an important role in nonviolent resistance?

2. In what ways do the white moderates pose the biggest stumbling block to equal rights for African Americans?

3. Do you agree with the oft-quoted line, "justice too long delayed is justice denied"? Explain.

Address to the Nation

BY JOHN F. KENNEDY

In June, 1963, even after the successes in Birmingham, the governor of Alabama, George Wallace, opposed the court-ordered admission of two African Americans to the University of Alabama. This blatant defiance of the law forced the federal government to act. On June 11, President Kennedy authorized the use of the army to desegregate the University of Alabama. That evening, the president gave a televised address to explain what the federal government was doing, to praise the Civil Rights movement, and to lay before the U.S. public his proposals for "securing the full constitutional rights of our citizens." Following is the text of Kennedy's address.

My fellow citizens.

This afternoon, following a series of threats and defiant statements, the presence of Alabama National Guardsmen was required on the University of Alabama to carry out the final and unequivocal order of the United States District Court of the Northern District of Alabama.

That order called for the admission of two clearly qualified young Alabama residents who happened to have been born Negro.

That they were admitted peacefully on the campus is due in good measure to the conduct of the students of the University of Alabama who met their responsibilities in a constructive way.

I hope that every American, regardless of where he lives, will stop and examine his conscience about this and other related incidents.

This nation was founded by men of many nations and backgrounds. It was founded on the principle that all men are created equal, and that the rights of every man are diminished when the rights of one man are threatened.

Today we are committed to a worldwide struggle to promote and protect the rights of all who wish to be free. And when Americans are sent to Vietnam or West Berlin we do not ask for whites only.

It ought to be possible, therefore, for American students of any color to attend any public institution they select without having to be backed up by troops. It ought to be possible for American consumers of any color to receive equal service in places of public accommodation, such as hotels and restaurants, and theaters and retail stores without being forced to resort to demonstrations in the street.

And it ought to be possible for American citizens of any color to register and to vote in a free election without interference or fear of **reprisal.**[1]

---

[1] **reprisal**—acts of retaliation.

It ought to be possible, in short, for every American to enjoy the privileges of being American without regard to his race or his color.

In short, every American ought to have the right to be treated as he would wish to be treated, as one would wish his children to be treated. But this is not the case.

The Negro baby born in America today, regardless of the section or the state in which he is born, has about one-half as much chance of completing high school as a white baby, born in the same place, on the same day; one-third as much chance of completing college; one-third as much chance of becoming a professional man; twice as much chance of becoming unemployed; about one-seventh as much chance of earning $10,000 a year; a life expectancy which is seven years shorter and the prospects of earning only half as much.

This is not a sectional issue. Difficulties over segregation and discrimination exist in every city, in every state of the Union, producing in many cities a rising tide of discontent that threatens the public safety.

Nor is this a **partisan**[2] issue. In a time of domestic crisis, men of goodwill and generosity should be able to unite regardless of party or politics.

This is not even a legal or legislative issue alone. It is better to settle these matters in the courts than on the streets, and new laws are needed at every level. But law alone cannot make men see right.

We are confronted primarily with a moral issue. It is as old as the Scriptures and is as clear as the American Constitution. The heart of the question is whether all Americans are to be afforded equal rights and equal opportunities; whether we are going to treat our fellow Americans as we want to be treated.

If an American, because his skin is dark, cannot eat lunch in a restaurant open to the public; if he cannot

---

[2] **partisan**—devoted to or biased in support of a party, group, or cause.

send his children to the best public school available; if he cannot vote for the public officials who represent him; if, in short, he cannot enjoy the full and free life which all of us want, then who among us would be content to have the color of his skin changed and stand in his place?

Who among us would then be content with the counsels of patience and delay? One hundred years of delay have passed since President Lincoln freed the slaves, yet their heirs, their grandsons, are not fully free. They are not yet freed from the bonds of injustice; they are not yet freed from social and economic oppression.

And this nation, for all its hopes and all its boasts, will not be fully free until all its citizens are free.

We preach freedom around the world, and we mean it. And we cherish our freedom here at home. But are we to say to the world—and much more importantly to each other—that this is the land of the free, except for the Negroes; that we have no second-class citizens, except Negroes; that we have no class or caste system, no ghettos, no master race, except with respect to Negroes?

Now the time has come for this nation to fulfill its promise. The events in Birmingham and elsewhere have so increased the cries for equality that no city or state or legislative body can prudently choose to ignore them.

The fires of frustration and discord are burning in every city, North and South. Where legal remedies are not at hand, **redress**[3] is sought in the streets in demonstrations, parades and protests, which create tensions and threaten violence—and threaten lives.

We face, therefore, a moral crisis as a country and a people. It cannot be met by repressive police action. It cannot be left to increased demonstrations in the streets. It cannot be quieted by token moves or talk. It is a time

---

[3] **redress**—satisfaction for wrong or injury; reparation.

to act in the Congress, in your state and local legislative body, and, above all, in all of our daily lives.

It is not enough to pin the blame on others, to say this is a problem of one section of the country or another, or deplore the facts that we face. A great change is at hand, and our task, our obligation, is to make that revolution, that change, peaceful and constructive for all.

Those who do nothing are inviting shame as well as violence. Those who act boldly are recognizing right as well as reality.

Next week I shall ask the Congress of the United States to act, to make a commitment it has not fully made in this century to the proposition that race has no place in American life or law.

The Federal judiciary has upheld that proposition in a series of forthright cases. The Executive Branch has adopted that proposition in the conduct of its affairs, including the employment of Federal personnel, and the use of Federal facilities, and the sale of Federally financed housing.

But there are other necessary measures which only the Congress can provide, and they must be provided at this session.

The old code of equity law under which we live commands for every wrong a remedy. But in too many communities, in too many parts of the country, wrongs are inflicted on Negro citizens and there are no remedies in law. Unless the Congress acts, their only remedy is the street.

I am, therefore, asking the Congress to enact legislation giving all Americans the right to be served in facilities which are open to the public—hotels, restaurants and theaters, retail stores and similar establishments. This seems to me to be an elementary right. Its denial is an arbitrary indignity that no American in 1963 should have to endure, but many do.

I have recently met with scores of business leaders, urging them to take voluntary action to end this discrimination. And I have been encouraged by their response. And in the last two weeks, over seventy-five cities have seen progress made in desegregating these kinds of facilities.

But many are unwilling to act alone. And for this reason nationwide legislation is needed, if we are to move this problem from the streets to the courts.

I am also asking Congress to authorize the Federal Government to participate more fully in lawsuits designed to end segregation in public education. We have succeeded in persuading many districts to desegregate voluntarily. Dozens have admitted Negroes without violence.

Today a Negro is attending a state-supported institution in every one of our fifty states. But the pace is very slow.

Too many Negro children entering segregated grade schools at the time of the Supreme Court's decision nine years ago will enter segregated high schools this fall, having suffered a loss which can never be restored.

The lack of an adequate education denies the Negro a chance to get a decent job. The orderly implementation of the Supreme Court decision, therefore, cannot be left solely to those who may not have the economic resources to carry their legal action or who may be subject to harassment. Other features will be also requested, including greater protection for the right to vote.

But legislation, I repeat, cannot solve this problem alone. It must be solved in the homes of every American in every community across our country.

In this respect, I want to pay tribute to those citizens, North and South, who have been working in their communities to make life better for all.

They are acting not out of a sense of legal duty but out of a sense of human decency. Like our soldiers and sailors in all parts of the world, they are meeting freedom's challenge on the firing line and I salute them for their honor—their courage.

My fellow Americans, this is a problem which faces us all, in every city of the North as well as the South.

Today there are Negroes unemployed—two or three times as many compared to whites; inadequate education; moving into the large cities, unable to find work; young people particularly out of work, without hope, denied equal rights, denied the opportunity to eat at a restaurant or a lunch counter, or go to a movie theater; denied the right to a decent education; denied almost, today, the right to attend a state university even though qualified.

It seems to me that these are matters which concern us all—not merely Presidents, or Congressmen, or Governors, but every citizen of the United States.

This is one country. It has become one country because all of us and all the people who came here had an equal chance to develop their talents.

We cannot say to ten percent of the population that "you can't have that right. Your children can't have the chance to develop whatever talents they have, that the only way that they are going to get their rights is to go in the street and demonstrate."

I think we owe them and we owe ourselves a better country than that.

QUESTIONS TO CONSIDER

1. What event or events prompted President Kennedy to make this speech?

2. What is the moral crisis that the country is facing?

3. What message does Kennedy have for those who have done nothing to help guarantee the rights of their African-American neighbors?

"I Have a Dream"

BY MARTIN LUTHER KING, JR.

*Late in 1962, two veteran Civil Rights leaders, A. Philip Randolph
and Bayard Rustin, had begun planning a large demonstration in
Washington, D.C. They wanted to hold a huge protest, not only to
press Congress and the President to enact Civil Rights legislation,
but also to celebrate the nonviolent philosophy of the movement.
On August 28, 1963, more than 200,000 people gathered at the
Washington Monument in the nation's capital and marched to the
Lincoln Memorial. Here they heard folk singers, such as Bob Dylan
and Joan Baez, sing "We Shall Overcome" (see page 92), and
listened to ten speakers. Martin Luther King, Jr., delivered the day's
triumphant oration, his celebrated "I Have a Dream" speech.*

I am happy to join with you today in what will go
down in history as the greatest demonstration for freedom in the history of our nation.

Fivescore years ago, a great American, in whose
symbolic shadow we stand today, signed the
Emancipation Proclamation. This momentous decree
came as a great beacon light of hope to millions of

Negro slaves who had been seared in the flames of withering injustice. It came as a joyous daybreak to end the long night of their captivity.

But one hundred years later, the Negro still is not free; one hundred years later, the life of the Negro is still sadly crippled by the **manacles**[1] of segregation and the chains of discrimination; one hundred years later, the Negro lives on a lonely island of poverty in the midst of a vast ocean of material prosperity; one hundred years later, the Negro is still languished in the corners of American society and finds himself in exile in his own land.

So we've come here today to dramatize a shameful condition. In a sense we've come to our nation's capital to cash a check. When the architects of our republic wrote the magnificent words of the Constitution and the Declaration of Independence, they were signing a promissory note to which every American was to fall heir. This note was the promise that all men, yes, black men as well as white men, would be guaranteed the unalienable rights of life, liberty, and the pursuit of happiness.

It is obvious today that America has defaulted on this promissory note in so far as her citizens of color are concerned. Instead of honoring this sacred obligation, America has given the Negro people a bad check; a check which has come back marked "insufficient funds." We refuse to believe that there are insufficient funds in the great vaults of opportunity of this nation. And so we've come to cash this check, a check that will give us upon demand the riches of freedom and the security of justice.

We have also come to this **hallowed**[2] spot to remind America of the fierce urgency of now. This is no time to engage in the luxury of cooling off or to take the

---

[1] **manacles**—shackles.

[2] **hallowed**—honored or revered.

tranquilizing drug of **gradualism**.[3] Now is the time to make real the promises of democracy; now is the time to rise from the dark and desolate valley of segregation to the sunlit path of racial justice; now is the time to lift our nation from the quicksands of racial injustice to the solid rock of brotherhood; now is the time to make justice a reality for all God's children. It would be fatal for the nation to overlook the urgency of the moment. This sweltering summer of the Negro's legitimate discontent will not pass until there is an invigorating autumn of freedom and equality.

Nineteen sixty-three is not an end, but a beginning. And those who hope that the Negro needed to blow off steam and will now be content, will have a rude awakening if the nation returns to business as usual.

There will be neither rest nor tranquility in America until the Negro is granted his citizenship rights. The whirlwinds of revolt will continue to shake the foundations of our nation until the bright day of justice emerges.

But there is something that I must say to my people who stand on the warm threshold which leads into the palace of justice. In the process of gaining our rightful place we must not be guilty of wrongful deeds.

Let us not seek to satisfy our thirst for freedom by drinking from the cup of bitterness and hatred. We must forever conduct our struggle on the high plane of dignity and discipline. We must not allow our creative protest to degenerate into physical violence. Again and again we must rise to the majestic heights of meeting physical force with soul force.

The marvelous new militancy which has engulfed the Negro community must not lead us to a distrust of all white people, for many of our white brothers, as evidenced by their presence here today, have come to realize that their destiny is tied up with our destiny and

---

[3] **gradualism**—the policy or principle of achieving something by gradual steps rather than by drastic change.

they have come to realize that their freedom is inextricably bound to our freedom. This offense we share mounted to storm the battlements of injustice must be carried forth by a biracial army. We cannot walk alone.

And as we walk, we must make the pledge that we shall always march ahead. We cannot turn back. There are those who are asking the devotees of civil rights, "When will you be satisfied?" We can never be satisfied as long as the Negro is the victim of the unspeakable horrors of police brutality.

We can never be satisfied as long as our bodies, heavy with fatigue of travel, cannot gain lodging in the motels of the highways and the hotels of the cities. We cannot be satisfied as long as the Negro's basic mobility is from a smaller ghetto to a larger one.

We can never be satisfied as long as our children are stripped of their selfhood and robbed of their dignity by signs stating "for whites only." We cannot be satisfied as long as a Negro in Mississippi cannot vote and a Negro in New York believes he has nothing for which to vote. No, we are not satisfied, and we will not be satisfied until justice rolls down like waters and righteousness like a mighty stream.

I am not unmindful that some of you have come here out of excessive trials and **tribulation.**[4] Some of you have come fresh from narrow jail cells. Some of you have come from areas where your quest for freedom left you battered by the storms of persecution and staggered by the winds of police brutality. You have been the veterans of creative suffering. Continue to work with the faith that unearned suffering is redemptive.

Go back to Mississippi; go back to Alabama; go back to South Carolina; go back to Georgia; go back to Louisiana; go back to the slums and ghettos of the northern cities, knowing that somehow this situation

---

[4] **tribulation**—great affliction, trial, or distress; suffering.

can, and will be changed. Let us not wallow in the valley of despair.

So I say to you, my friends, that even though we must face the difficulties of today and tomorrow, I still have a dream. It is a dream deeply rooted in the American dream that one day this nation will rise up and live out the true meaning of its **creed**[5]— we hold these truths to be self-evident, that all men are created equal.

I have a dream that one day on the red hills of Georgia, sons of former slaves and sons of former slave-owners will be able to sit down together at the table of brotherhood.

I have a dream that one day, even the state of Mississippi, a state sweltering with the heat of injustice, sweltering with the heat of oppression, will be transformed into an oasis of freedom and justice.

I have a dream my four little children will one day live in a nation where they will not be judged by the color of their skin but by content of their character. I have a dream today!

I have a dream that one day, down in Alabama, with its vicious racists, with its governor having his lips dripping with the words of **interposition**[6] and **nullification**,[7] that one day, right there in Alabama, little black boys and black girls will be able to join hands with little white boys and white girls as sisters and brothers. I have a dream today!

I have a dream that one day every valley shall be exalted, every hill and mountain shall be made low, the rough places shall be made plain, and the crooked places shall be made straight and the glory of the Lord will be revealed and all flesh shall see it together.

---

[5] **creed**—guiding principle.

[6] **interposition**—interference.

[7] **nullification**—invalidation.

This is our hope. This is the faith that I go back to the South with.

With this faith we will be able to hear out of the mountain of despair a stone of hope. With this faith we will be able to transform the jangling discords of our nation into a beautiful symphony of brotherhood.

With this faith we will be able to work together, to pray together, to struggle together, to go to jail together, to stand up for freedom together, knowing that we will be free one day. This will be the day when all of God's children will be able to sing with new meaning—"my country 'tis of thee; sweet land of liberty; of thee I sing; land where my fathers died, land of the pilgrim's pride; from every mountain side, let freedom ring"—and if America is to be a great nation, this must become true.

So let freedom ring from the prodigious hilltops of New Hampshire.

Let freedom ring from the mighty mountains of New York.

Let freedom ring from the heightening Alleghenies of Pennsylvania.

Let freedom ring from the snow-capped Rockies of Colorado.

Let freedom ring from the curvaceous slopes of California.

But not only that.

Let freedom ring from Stone Mountain of Georgia.

Let freedom ring from Lookout Mountain of Tennessee.

Let freedom ring from every hill and molehill of Mississippi, from every mountainside, let freedom ring.

And when we allow freedom to ring, when we let it ring from every village and hamlet, from every state and city, we will be able to speed up that day when all of God's children—black men and white men, Jews and

Gentiles, Catholics and Protestants—will be able to join hands and to sing in the words of the old Negro spiritual, "Free at last, free at last; thank God Almighty, we are free at last."

QUESTIONS TO CONSIDER

1. What is the "bad check" that Dr. King says America has given its African-American citizens?

2. In paragraph six, King issues an explicit warning to the American people. What is it?

3. What would you say is the emotional effect of this speech?

Attacked in Anniston Freedom Riders sit outside their burned-out bus, which was bombed by a white mob in Anniston, Alabama. ▶

Freedom Rides Freedom Riders sing as their bus pulls into a segregated city in the South.
▼

The Movement Spreads

▲

Sit-in Ronald Martin, Robert Patterson, and Mark Martin stage a sit-in at a Woolworth's lunch counter in Greensboro, North Carolina.

▲
Protesters Integrated protesters march in support of Martin Luther King, Jr.

▲

Birmingham An African-American woman is arrested during the protests in Birmingham, Alabama.

Birmingham Marchers Protesters draw attention to Martin Luther King, Jr.'s arrest in Birmingham, Alabama. ▶

March on Washington Protesters fill the park at the Lincoln Memorial on August 28, 1963.

▲

Marchers Gather All the marchers gather to hear speeches by the
Civil Rights movement's greatest leaders.

▲
I Have A Dream Martin Luther King, Jr., who delivered the famous speech at the March on Washington.

chapter four

Tragedy and
Triumph

Freedom Schools

The Student Nonviolent Coordinating Committee (SNCC) decided to make a huge push in Mississippi in 1964 in a summer campaign that would be known as "Freedom Summer." The idea was that hundreds of volunteers would pour into Mississippi and work to get African Americans registered to vote and to set up "Freedom Schools," which would teach basic skills and their own history to African-American children. "Freedom Summer" was the apex of the nonviolent movement for civil rights, and during the course of the summer hundreds of thousands of Mississippians had their lives touched and improved. In the following two selections, Fannie Lou Hamer describes registering to vote in testimony at the Democratic National Convention on August 22, 1964, and Liz Fusco describes the Freedom Schools and reprints student poetry.

Testimony of Fannie Lou Hamer

Mr. Chairman, and the Credentials Committee, my name is Mrs. Fannie Lou Hamer, and I live at 626 East Lafayette Street, Ruleville, Mississippi, Sunflower

County, the home of Senator James O. Eastland, and Senator Stennis.

It was the 31st of August in 1962 that 18 of us traveled 26 miles to the county courthouse in Indianola to try to register to try to become first-class citizens. We was met in Indianola by Mississippi men, Highway Patrolmen and they allowed two of us in to take the literacy test at the time. After we had taken the test and started back to Ruleville, we was held up by the City Police and the State Highway Patrolmen and carried back to Indianola where the bus driver was charged that day with driving a bus the wrong color.

After we paid the fine among us, we continued on to Ruleville, and Reverend Jeff Sunny carried me the four miles in the rural area where I had worked as a time-keeper and sharecropper for 18 years. I was met there by my children, who told me the plantation owner was angry because I had gone down to try to register.

After they told me, my husband came, and said the plantation owner was raising cain because I had tried to register and before he quit talking the plantation owner came, and said, "Fannie Lou, do you know—did Pap tell you what I said?" And I said, "Yes sir." He said, "I mean that . . . If you don't go down and withdraw . . . well—you might have to go because we are not ready for that. . . . "

And I addressed him and told him and said, "I didn't try to register for you. I tried to register for myself."

I had to leave that same night.

On the 10th of September, 1962, 16 bullets was fired into the home of Mr. and Mrs. Robert Tucker for me. That same night two girls were shot in Ruleville, Mississippi. Also Mr. Joe McDonald's house was shot in.

And in June, the 9th, 1963, I had attended a voter registration workshop, was returning back to Mississippi. Ten of us was traveling by the Continental Trailways bus. When we got to Winona, Mississippi, which is Montgomery County, four of the people got off to use the washroom. . . . I stepped off the bus to see what was happening and somebody screamed from the car that four workers was in and said, "Get that one there," and when I went to get in the car, when the man told me I was under arrest, he kicked me.

I was carried to the county jail and put in the holding room. They left some of the people in the booking room and began to place us in cells. I was placed in a cell with a young woman called Miss Euvester Simpson. After I was placed in the cell I began to hear sounds of licks and screams. I could hear the sounds of licks and horrible screams, and I could hear somebody say, "Can you say, yes, sir, [racial epithet]?" "Can you say yes, sir?"

And they would say horrible names. She would say. "Yes, I can say yes, sir" . . . They beat her, I don't know how long, and after a while she began to pray and asked God to have Mercy on those people. And it wasn't too long before three white men came to my cell. One of these men was a State Highway Patrolman and he asked me where I was from, and I told him Ruleville; he said, "We are going to check this."

And they left my cell and it wasn't too long before they came back. He said, "You are from Ruleville all right," and he used a curse word, he said, "We are going to beat you until you wish you was dead."

I was carried out of that cell into another cell where they had two Negro prisoners. The State Highway patrolmen ordered the first Negro to take the blackjack. The first Negro prisoner ordered me, by orders from the State Highway Patrolmen, for me to lay down on a bunk bed on my face, and I laid on my face.

The first Negro began to beat, and I was beat by the first Negro until he was exhausted, and I was holding my hands behind at this time on my left side because I suffered polio when I was six years old. After the first Negro had beat until he was exhausted the state Highway Patrolman ordered the second Negro to take the blackjack. The second Negro began to beat and I began to work my feet, and the State Highway Patrolmen ordered the first Negro who had beat to set on my feet to keep me from working my feet. I began to scream and one white man got up and began to beat me in my head and tell me to hush. . . .

All of this on account we want to register, to become first-class citizens, and if the freedom Democratic Party is not seated now, I question America, is this America, the land of the free and the home of the brave where we have to sleep with our telephones off the hooks because our lives be threatened daily because we want to live as decent human beings, in America?

from Deeper Than Politics
by Liz Fusco

The original plan for Freedom Schools developed from Charles Cobb's dream that what could be done in Mississippi could be deeper, more fundamental, more far-reaching, more revolutionary than voter registration alone: more personal, and in a sense more transforming, than a political program. The validity of the dream is evidenced by the fact that people trying desperately to keep alive while working on voter registration could take seriously the idea that Mississippi needs more than for Negroes to have the right to vote.

The decision to have Freedom Schools in Mississippi seems to have been a decision, then, to enter into every phase of the lives of the people of Mississippi. It seems to have been a decision to set the people free for politics in the only way that people can become live and that is totally. . . .

The so-called "Citizenship Curriculum" set up two sets of questions. The "primary" set was: (1) Why are we (teachers and students) in Freedom Schools? (2) What is the Freedom Movement? (3) What alternative does the Freedom Movement offer us? The "secondary" set of questions (which seemed to me more important because more personal) was: (1) What does the majority culture have that we want? (2) What does the majority culture have that we don't want? (3) What do we have that we want to keep?

The continual raising of these questions in many contexts may be said to be what the Freedom Schools were about. This was so because in order to answer them it was necessary for the students to confront other questions of who he is, what his world is like, and how he fits into or is alienated from it. . . .

The kids began to see two things at once: that the North was no real escape, and that the South was not some vague white monster doomed irrationally to crush them. Simultaneously, they began to discover that they themselves could take action against injustices which have kept them unhappy and **impotent**.[1]

Through the study of Negro history they began to have a true sense of themselves as a people who could produce heroes. . . .

---

[1] **impotent**—lacking in power; helpless.

I Am Mississippi Fed

BY IDA RUTH GRIFFIN, AGE 12, HARMONY, CARTHAGE

I am Mississippi fed, I am Mississippi bred, Nothing
but a poor, black boy.
I am a Mississippi slave, I shall be buried in a
Mississippi grave,
Nothing but a poor, dead boy.

Fight On Little Children

BY EDITH MOORE, AGE 15, McCOMB

Fight on little children, fight on
You know what you're doing is right.
Don't stop, keep straight ahead
You're just bound to win the fight.
Many hardships there will be;
Many trials you'll have to face.
But go on children, keep fighting
Soon freedom will take hardship's place.
Sometimes it's going to be hard;
Sometimes the light will look dim.
But keep it up, don't get discouraged
Keep fighting, though chances seem slim.
In the end you and I know
That one day the fact they'll face.
And realize we're human too
That freedom's taken slavery's place

Freedom in Mississippi

BY DAVID MARCH, AGE 16, INDIANOLA

In the middle of the night,
a stressive bell of Hope is ringing
Everyone is on the eve of fear and success
is not yet come
Until Everyone Wakes up and Speaks out
in an overcoming voice, the slums will Remain.
Let Not the pulling out of a few
go down the whole crowd.
If this remains we will forever be
under bowed.

Mr. Turnbow

BY LORENZO WESLEY, MILESTONE

I know a man who has no foe
His name is Mr. Turnbow
He is about five feet six
Every time you see him he has a gun or a brick.
If you want to keep your head
Then you'd better not come tripping around his bed.
When he talks to you
His fingers talk too.
Some people will never understand
But Mr. Turnbow is a good old man.

Mine

BY ALICE JACKSON, AGE 17, JACKSON

I want to walk the streets of town
Turn into any restaurant and sit down
And be served the food of my choice,
And not be met by a hostile voice.
I want to live in the best hotel for a week,
Or go for a swim at a public beach.
I want to go to the best University
and not be met with violence or uncertainty.
I want the things my ancestors
thought we'd never have.
They are mine as a Negro, an American;
I shall have them or be dead.

QUESTIONS TO CONSIDER

1. What are some of the indignities Fannie Lou Hamer suffered because she wanted the right to vote?

2. What was the purpose of the Freedom Schools?

3. Reread the Freedom School poems. Would you say these poets feel optimistic that their world will change for the better? Use lines from the poems to support your answer.

from

Three Lives for Mississippi

BY WILLIAM BRADFORD HUIE

Before the campaigns of the "Freedom Summer" began in 1964, all the volunteers and activists met in Oxford, Mississippi. It was here that they discovered that three activists, James Chaney, Michael Schwerner, and Andrew Goodman were missing. When their disappearance was reported, Mississippi officials refused to do anything. The FBI, however, undertook a massive manhunt and on August 4 uncovered the bodies of the three. They had been murdered at the time of their disappearance and dumped in an earthen dam outside Philadelphia, Mississippi. In the following selection, investigator William Bradford Huie describes how the three were murdered and their bodies disposed of. This incident was the basis for the movie Mississippi Burning.

When the three were ordered or pulled from the station wagon, I think they must have been placed in handcuffs, though I was told that they were not. "They were still following orders," I was told, "and Schwerner and Goodman still didn't think they were going to be killed. They thought they were going to be whipped."

I was told that James Chaney recognized one of the men from Meridian, called him by name, and asked him for help.

The murder was done in the "cut" on Rock Cut Road, less than a mile from Highway 19, about four miles from where the three were taken from the station wagon. It was before midnight, and the moon was still high. Three cars were in the cut. I was told that the three victims said nothing, but that they were jeered by the murderers. Several of the murderers chanted in unison, as though they had practiced it:

"Ashes to ashes, Dust to dust, If you'd stayed where you belonged, You wouldn't be here with us."

When Schwerner was pulled from the car and stood up to be shot, I was told that the man with the pistol asked him: "You still think a [racial epithet] is as good as I am?" No time was allowed for a reply. He was shot straight through the heart and fell to the ground.

Goodman was next, with nothing said. Apparently he stood as still as Schwerner did, facing his executioner, for the shot that killed him was the same precise shot. I was told that another man fired the shot, using the same pistol, but my opinion remains that one man fired both shots. I also still believe that both Schwerner and Goodman were in handcuffs, and that the cuffs were removed after they were dead.

Chaney was last, and the only difference was that he struggled while the others had not. He didn't stand still; he tried to pull and duck away from his executioner. So he wasn't shot with the same precision, and he was shot three times instead of once.

Because Chaney's wrist, shoulder, and skull were crushed, a reputable New York doctor who examined Chaney's body said that he had been beaten, perhaps with a chain. Certainly the murderers were capable of it: they were capable of anything. But I would guess that it didn't happen, though he certainly could have been badly hurt in the struggle. All three bodies were buried in darkness with a bulldozer. The bulldozers could easily have done additional damage to Chaney.

The federal indictment concerned with these murders charges that the three were let out of jail about 10:30 P.M., and that they were murdered on June 21, 1964. This means that federal agents are convinced that the murder was done before midnight. So these murders were committed with **dispatch.**[1] There was no horsing around, or "interrogation," or torture, as in the case of Edward Aaron. When white-supremacy terrorists are bent on murder they seldom pause to torture. And they usually hate "[racial epithet]-lovers" more than they hate "[racial epithet]." Which is why I think that—if they were going to single out a victim and beat him—Schwerner, not Chaney, would have been the preferred choice.

The three bodies were tossed into the station wagon and driven along dirt roads to a farm about six miles southwest of Philadelphia. A "cattle pond" was under construction on this farm. There are scores of such ponds in Neshoba County. A pond is created by erecting an earthen dam in a proper spot. To begin building a dam you generally dig a ditch maybe 30 feet wide and 5 feet deep and 100 or more feet long. Into this ditch you pack red clay; it hardens, and creates a base for the dam under which water will not seep. Onto this base you then pile dirt, sloping the sides, to whatever height is needed. You plant grass along the sides. A finished dam may be 30 feet wide at the base, 10 feet wide at the top, 20 feet high, and 100 feet long, all erected on the red-clay base.

---

[1] **dispatch**—with promptness or speed.

Such a dam is a perfect place in which to hide bodies. On June 21 only the red-clay base had been built, and a bulldozer was parked at the scene. One of the conspirators operated the bulldozer. He was supposed to be waiting for the murderers, but he was late. They arrived before he did, and they had to wait almost two hours for him. The moon went down behind the trees. This wait must have been unpleasant, even for such patriots proud of their courage, and I was told that a gallon of corn whiskey was delivered to them to help them through their bloody wake. Many good stories must have been told, to cackling and thigh-slapping, during that two hours of drinking and waiting at the lonely construction site.

During the Second World War I remember seeing dead soldiers buried temporarily with bulldozers. We did this at Omaha Beach. Many Americans saw this done, and I suspect it was one such old veteran who thought of playing hide-and-seek with the agents of the United States by burying these bodies with a bulldozer.

When the bulldozer operator arrived, he dug a trench in the red clay along the length of the dam. The bodies, fully clothed, were tossed into this trench, face down, side by side. Goodman and Schwerner were head to head and feet to feet; Chaney, on the outside, was in the opposite position: his feet were at Schwerner's head. The two white men's arms were above their heads, indicating that they were dropped into the dirt by one man holding wrists and another holding ankles. Chaney's arms were at his sides, probably because his wrist was broken, so he would have been carried or dragged by his armpits. The bodies were then covered with two feet of dirt, and in subsequent weeks the dam was built to a height of eighteen feet. Heavy rains fell during July; so by August first the dam was massive and grassed over—a permanent tomb for three bodies if nobody ever talked.

After the burial the station wagon was driven to a point fifteen miles northeast of Philadelphia, to the edge of the Bogue Chitto swamp. There it was doused with diesel fuel and burned. The murderers thought this was clever, almost as clever as burying the bodies in the dam. They knew that only federal agents—no one else—would ever search for the bodies; so each move they made was part of a fascinating game they thought they were playing with the FBI.

Traditionally in race murders bodies have been thrown into rivers and swamps in Mississippi. So the murderers, by burning the station wagon on the edge of Bogue Chitto swamp, were leading the "federals" to begin by dragging the rivers and swamps. And the murderers thought this was funny because it was hot summertime and the swamps and rivers were teeming with snakes, chiggers, and mosquitoes.

"It tickles the hell out of me," one of the murderers said, "just to think of old J. Edgar's boys sweatin' out there in that swamp, with all them chiggers, water moccasins, and skeeters."

Since the bodies were buried six miles *southwest* of Philadelphia, and the station wagon was burned fifteen miles *northeast* of Philadelphia, this meant that the search would begin twenty-one miles from where the bodies were; and by the time all the rivers and swamps were searched, the dam would be completed and grassed over.

Shortly before the early dawn, the murderers had finished all their chores tidily, and the last group of them gathered on the courthouse square in Philadelphia to shake hands and congratulate one another. They all had been drinking though none could be called drunk. There they were met by an official of the state of Mississippi.

"Well, boys," he said, "you've done a good job. You've struck a blow for the White Man. Mississippi can be proud of you. You've let these agitatin' Outsiders know where this state stands. Go home now and forget it. But before you go, I'm looking each one of you in the eye and telling you this: the first man who talks is *dead!* If anybody who knows anything about this ever opens his mouth to any Outsider about it, then the rest of us are going to kill him just as dead as we killed those [expletive] tonight.

"Does everybody understand what I'm saying? The man who talks is dead . . . dead . . . *dead!*" . . .

QUESTIONS TO CONSIDER

1. Why are the three men murdered? Who committed the crime?

2. Why do you think the killers enjoyed playing games with the FBI?

3. According to the official, what "stand" was made by the state of Mississippi the night Schwerner, Goodman, and Chaney were killed?

Violence and Voter Registration

The 1964 Civil Rights Act prohibited discrimination in voter registra-
tion. In 1965, Martin Luther King, Jr., launched a massive voter
registration drive, leading 400 African Americans to the Selma,
Alabama, courthouse where they were turned away by policemen
with clubs and cattle prods. Over the next seven weeks, these
marches continued and thousands of African Americans were arrested.
The protests spread throughout the cities around Selma, and on
March 2, at a rally in nearby Marion, Alabama, a mob of white
policemen and civilians attacked peaceful marchers, brutally murder-
ing one. King called for a march from Selma to Alabama's capital
of Montgomery on March 7. As the marchers prepared to leave
Selma, they were met on the Edmund Pettus Bridge by a mob of
state troopers and local policemen. The marchers were attacked
with tear gas, clubs, and whips. In the following selections, Willie
Bolden describes the attack in Marion, and Sheyann Webb describes
the attack on the Pettus Bridge.

Willie Bolden's Recollections

I spoke and was not really anticipating a march that night. . . . Most people who speak will say that if you can get to yourself, you know that you are getting to others, and out of the clear blue, at the end of my speech, I asked how many people would like to have a march. Every living soul in that church stood up. So we began to move, the three guys who I brought with me, the preacher from their church, I believe, and some other ladies who participated on the program. I filed out, off the pulpit, down the aisle, and when I got outside, we turned to the right because the courthouse was directly across the street, and we were going to march around there, and I was going to give another little **spiel**[1] at the courthouse. The cameras were shooting, and all of a sudden, out of nowhere, we heard cameras being broken, newspapermen being hit, and looked around and saw folk trying to run out of the church. And what they had done, they had gone through the side and the back of the church, and the troopers were in there beating folk . . . trying to get 'em out, and troopers were outside along with the local police and sheriff department, beating folk out there. Okay? I'll never forget this night.

A big, white cop—well, a big white fella in a suit—came up to me—I was still in the front of the march—and stuck a double-barrel shotgun, cocked, in my stomach and said, "You're the [racial epithet] from Atlanta, aren't you?" And I said, "Yes." He said, "Somebody want to see you across the street." Now, while all of this was going on, people were still getting beaten. Okay? So he took me across the street, and there was a guy standing there who claimed to have been the sheriff, and I think he was because of his badge, with some red suspenders and chewing tobacco and one of those big hats on. Said, "Now, you see what you

---

[1] **spiel**—speech; talk.

caused." And I said, "How did I do that?" He said, "Because if you had kept yo' black [expletive] in Atlanta, this would not have happened." I said, "I didn't come here from Atlanta. I came here from Selma, Alabama." He said, "If you had stayed there, this would not have happened." I said, "The Constitution gives us the right to peacefully protest whatever grievance we might have." He said, "You don't have any constitutional rights in my town." I said, "Yeah, so I see." At that time, folks were still getting beaten.

He grabbed me by the coat and spin me around, and he said, "I just want you to watch this." Folk were running over each other and trying to protect themselves. So I began to cry, 'cause it was just . . . you had to see it . . . it was just, just . . . you could just see folks grabbing their heads. And one guy was running over toward in our direction, and he saw the polices standin' there by the sheriff, and he tried to make a turn, and when he did, he ran into one of those local cops, and they hit him in the head, and it just bust his head wide open. Blood spewed all over, and he fell. And I tried to get over there to him, and the sheriff pulled me back, and I turned around to say something to him, and when I turned around he stuck a .38 snubnose right in my mouth. He said, "What you gon' say?" I said, "I ain't gon' say nothin'." You know, what the hell you gonna say?

He cocked the hammer back, and he said, "What I really need to do is blow your [expletive] brains out, [racial epithet]." Of course, I didn't say nothin'. I was *scared to death*, and all I could see was those rounds in that chamber.[2] He said, "Take this [racial epithet] over there to the jail." The jail was right up the street from the church and right across the street from the courthouse. So they took me over there, and in taking me over there, the guy just hit me all over the arm, legs, thighs, and the

---

[2] rounds in that chamber—ammunition in the part of the gun that holds the charge.

chin, really did me in kind of bad. And when I walked in the door, there was blood on the floor. Just literally puddles of blood leading all the way up the stairs to the jail cell. And when I got up there, folk were hollering, "I need a doctor, I need a doctor, I need a doctor." And nobody paid any attention to 'em. And when the guy opened the cell where I was to push me in, two of 'em caught me at the same time side the head there. The only thing probably saved me a little bit was when the first guy hit me and the other one attempted to hit me, all his billy club did was hit the stick that was already here, so I got a kinda double jog, bip-bip. Had a little hickey up there, and when they pushed me in, my forehead hit the top bunk in the thing, and I had a big knot there.

Shortly after I was in there, that's when we heard the shots. Well, that's when Jimmie Lee Jackson got killed. The cop was beating on his mama, and he was headed toward his mother, and that's when they shot him. 'Course, I never read anything like that in these books and things that I've read about the Civil Rights Movement and why Jimmie Lee Jackson was killed or how he got killed. Much of what I told you, I have never read in a book period about what took place at a particular situation. I am inclined to believe that they got their information either from the paper or tried to analyze some filmstrips on what happened. Even in filming, in many cases, they missed a lot of it because if the [expletive] was gonna *really* go down, those folk tried to get those cameras out of the way first. And many times even after they were able to put the camera back into motion, much of the real *bloody* part of these marches was all over.

from **Selma, Lord, Selma**

by Sheyann Webb

Now the Edmund Pettus Bridge sits above the downtown; you have to walk up it like it's a hill. We couldn't see the other side, we couldn't see the troopers. So we started up and the first part of the line was over. I couldn't see all that much because I was so little; the people in front blocked my view.

But when we got up there on that high part and looked down we saw them. I remember the woman [next to her] saying something like, "Oh, My Lord" or something. And I stepped out to the side for a second and I saw them. They were in a line—they looked like a blue picket fence stretched across the highway. There were others gathered behind that first line and to the sides, along the little service road in front of the stores and drive-ins, there was a group of white people. And further back were some of Sheriff Jim Clark's possemen on their horses. Traffic had been blocked.

At that point I began to get a little uneasy about things. I think everyone did. People quit talking; it was so quiet then that all you could hear was the wind blowing and our footsteps on the concrete sidewalk.

Well, we kept moving down the bridge. I remember glancing at the water in the Alabama River, and it was yellow and looked cold. I was told later that Hosea Williams said to John Lewis, "See that water down there? I hope you can swim, 'cause we're fixin' to end up in it."

The troopers could be seen more clearly now. I guess I was fifty to seventy-five yards from them. They were wearing blue helmets, blue jackets, and they carried clubs in their hands; they had those gas-mask pouches slung across their shoulders. The first part of the march line reached them and we all came to a stop. For a few seconds we just kept standing, and then I heard this voice speaking over the bullhorn saying that this was an unlawful assembly and for us to disperse and go back to the church.

I remember I held the woman's hand who was next to me and had it gripped hard. I wasn't really scared at that point. Then I stepped out a way and looked again and saw the troopers putting on their masks. That scared me. I had never faced the troopers before, and nobody had ever put on gas masks during the downtown marches. But this one was different; we were out of the city limits and on a highway. Williams said something to the troopers asking if we could pray—I didn't hear it but was told later that we could—and then I heard the voice again come over the bullhorn and tell us we had two minutes to disperse.

Some of the people around me began to talk then, saying something about, "Get ready, we're going to jail," words to that effect.

But I didn't know about that; the masks scared me. So the next thing I know—it didn't seem like two minutes had gone by—the voice was saying, "Troopers advance and see that they are dispersed." Just all of a sudden it was beginning to happen. I couldn't see for sure how it began, but just before it did I took another look and saw this line of troopers moving toward us; the wind was whipping at their pant legs. . . .

All I knew is I heard all this screaming and the people were turning and I saw this first part of the line running and stumbling back toward us. At that point, I was just off the bridge and on the side of the highway. And they came running and some of them were crying out and somebody yelled, "Oh, God, they're killing us!" I think I just froze then. There were people everywhere, jamming against me, pushing against me. Then, all of a sudden, it stopped and everyone got down on their knees, and I did too, and somebody was saying for us to pray. But there was so much excitement it never got started, because everybody was talking and they were scared and we didn't know what was happening or was going to happen. I remember looking toward the troopers and they were backing up, but some of them were standing over some of our people who had been knocked down or had fallen. It seemed like just a few seconds went by and I heard a shout. "Gas! Gas!" And everybody started screaming again. And I looked and I saw the troopers charging us again and some of them were swinging their arms and throwing canisters of tear gas. And beyond them I saw the horsemen starting their charge toward us. I was terrified. What happened then is something I'll never forget as long as I live. Never. In fact, I still dream about it sometimes.

I saw those horsemen coming toward me and they had those awful masks on; they rode right through the cloud of gas. Some of them had clubs, others had ropes or whips, which they swung about them like they were driving cattle. I'll tell you, I forgot about praying, and I just turned and ran. And just as I was turning the tear gas got me; it burned my nose first and then got my eyes. I was blinded by tears. So I began running and not seeing where I was going. I remember being scared that I might fall over the railing and into the water. I don't know if I was screaming or not, but everyone else was. . . . It was like a nightmare seeing it through the tears. I just knew then that I was going to die, that those horses were going to trample me. So I kind of knelt down and held my hands and arms up over my head. . . .

All of a sudden somebody was grabbing me under the arms and lifting me up and running. The horses went by and I kept waiting to get trampled on or hit, but they went on by and I guess they were hitting at somebody else. And I looked up and saw it was Hosea Williams who had me and he was running but we didn't seem to be moving, and I kept kicking my legs in the air, trying to speed up, and I shouted at him, "Put me down! You can't run fast enough with me!"

But he held on until we were off the bridge and down on Broad Street and he let me go. I didn't stop running until I got home. All along the way there were people running in small groups; I saw people jumping over cars and being chased by the horsemen who kept hitting them. . . .

When I got into the house my momma and daddy were there and they had this shocked look on their faces and I ran in and tried to tell them what had happened. I was maybe a little hysterical because I kept repeating over and over, "I can't stop shaking, Momma, I can't stop shaking," and finally she grabbed me and sat down with me on her lap. But my daddy was like I'd never seen him before. He had a shotgun and yelled. "By God, if they want it this way, I'll give it to them!" And he started out the door. Momma jumped up and got in front of him shouting at him. And he said, "I'm ready to die; I mean it! I'm ready to die!" I was crying on the couch, I was so scared. But finally he put the gun aside and sat down. I remember just laying there on the couch, crying and feeling so disgusted. They had beaten us like we were slaves.

QUESTIONS TO CONSIDER

1. Who does Willie Bolden seem to blame most for the atrocities in Marion?

2. Why, according to Bolden, are stories like his usually missing from books about the Civil Rights movement?

3. What did you find most disturbing about Sheyann Webb's story?

Speech to Congress

"And We Shall Overcome"

BY LYNDON B. JOHNSON

On July 2, 1964, Congress finally passed, after a year of wrangling, the Civil Rights Act. This bill prohibited discrimination in voting, employment, and public facilities. Still, the bill had been greatly watered down in Congress and left many Civil Rights advocates disappointed. One was President Lyndon Johnson, and in the wake of the shocking violence in Selma, Alabama, Johnson gave a nationally televised speech on March 15, 1965. He called on each and every American to fight "to overcome the crippling legacy of bigotry and injustice." No president before Johnson had made the issue of integration a key national issue. In August, Johnson was able to sign into law the Voting Rights Act, which prohibited discriminatory tests in voter registration and provided for federal examiners to add African Americans to the voting rolls in the South. Within a year, more than 450,000 African Americans had registered to vote.

I speak tonight for the dignity of man and the destiny of democracy.

I urge every member of both parties, Americans of all religions and of all colors, from every section of this country, to join me in that cause.

At times history and fate meet at a single time in a single place to shape a turning point in man's unending search for freedom. So it was at Lexington and Concord. So it was a century ago at Appomattox. So it was last week in Selma, Alabama.

There, long-suffering men and women peacefully protested the denial of their rights as Americans. Many were brutally assaulted. One good man, a man of God, was killed.

There is no cause for pride in what has happened in Selma. There is no cause for self-satisfaction in the long denial of equal rights to millions of Americans. But there is cause for hope and for faith in our democracy in what is happening here tonight.

For the cries of pain and the hymns and protests of oppressed people have summoned into **convocation**[1] all the majesty of this great government of the greatest nation on earth.

Our mission is at once the oldest and the most basic of this country: to right wrong, to do justice, to serve man.

In our time we have come to live with moments of great crisis. Our lives have been marked with debate about great issues; issues of war and peace, of prosperity and depression. But rarely in any time does an issue lay bare the secret heart of America itself. Rarely are we met with a challenge, not to our growth or abundance, our welfare or our security, but rather to the values and the purposes and the meaning of our beloved nation.

The issue of equal rights for American Negroes is such an issue. And should we defeat every enemy,

---

[1] **convocation**—the act or process of calling together.

should we double our wealth and conquer the stars, and still be unequal to this issue, then we will have failed as a people and as a nation.

For with a country as with a person, "What is a man profited, if he shall gain the whole world, and lose his own soul?"

There is no Negro problem. There is no Southern problem. There is no Northern problem. There is only an American problem. And we are met here tonight as Americans to solve that problem.

This was the first nation in the history of the world to be founded with a purpose. The great phrases of that purpose still sound in every American heart, North and South: "All men are created equal," "government by consent of the governed," "give me liberty or give me death." Those are not just clever words. Those are not just empty theories. In their name Americans have fought and died for two centuries, and tonight around the world they stand there as guardians of our liberty, risking their lives.

Those words are a promise to every citizen that he shall share in the dignity of man. This dignity cannot be found in a man's possessions, his power or his position. It rests on his right to be treated as a man equal in opportunity to all others. It says that he shall share in freedom, choose his leaders, educate his children, and provide for his family according to his ability and his merits as a human being.

To apply any other test—to deny a man his hopes because of his color or race, his religion or the place of his birth—is not only to do injustice, it is to deny America and to dishonor the dead who gave their lives for American freedom.

Our fathers believed that if this noble view of the rights of man was to flourish, it must be rooted in democracy. The most basic right of all was the right to choose your own leaders. The history of this country, in large measure, is the history of the expansion of that right to all of our people.

Many of the issues of civil rights are very complex and most difficult. But about this there can and should be no argument. Every American citizen must have an equal right to vote. There is no reason which can excuse the denial of that right. There is no duty which weighs more heavily on us than the duty we have to ensure that right.

Yet the harsh fact is that in many places in this country men and women are kept from voting simply because they are Negroes.

Every device of which human ingenuity is capable has been used to deny this right. The Negro citizen may go to register only to be told that the day is wrong, or the hour is late, or the official in charge is absent. And if he persists, and if he manages to present himself to the registrar, he may be disqualified because he did not spell out his middle name or because he abbreviated a word on the application.

And if he manages to fill out an application he is given a test. The registrar is the sole judge of whether he passes this test. He may be asked to recite the entire constitution, or explain the most complex provisions of state laws. And even a college degree cannot be used to prove that he can read and write.

For the fact is that the only way to pass these barriers is to show a white skin.

Experience has clearly shown that the existing process of law cannot overcome systematic and ingenious discrimination. No law that we now have on the books—and I have helped to put three of them there—can ensure the right to vote when local officials are determined to deny it.

In such a case our duty must be clear to all of us. The Constitution says that no person shall be kept from voting because of his race or his color. We have all sworn an oath before God to support and to defend that Constitution. We must now act in obedience to that oath.

Wednesday I will send to Congress a law designed to eliminate illegal barriers to the right to vote.

The broad principle of that bill will be in the hands of the Democratic and Republican leaders tomorrow. After they have reviewed it, it will come here formally as a bill. I am grateful for this opportunity to come here tonight at the invitation of the leadership to reason with my friends, to give them my views, and to visit with my former colleagues.

I have had prepared a more comprehensive analysis of the legislation which I intended to transmit tomorrow but which I will submit to the clerks tonight. But I want to discuss with you now briefly the main proposals of this legislation.

This bill will strike down restrictions to voting in all elections—Federal, State, and local—which have been used to deny Negroes the right to vote.

This bill will establish a simple, uniform standard which cannot be used, however ingenious the effort, to **flout**[2] our Constitution.

It will provide for citizens to be registered by officials of the United States government if the State officials refuse to register them.

It will eliminate tedious, unnecessary lawsuits which delay the right to vote.

Finally, this legislation will ensure that properly registered individuals are not prohibited from voting.

I will welcome suggestions from all of the members of Congress—and I have no doubt that I will get some—on ways and means to strengthen this law and to make it effective. But experience has plainly shown that this is the only path to carry out the command of the Constitution.

---

[2] **flout**—insult; mock.

To those who seek to avoid action by their national government in their own communities; who seek to maintain purely local control over elections, the answer is simple:

Open your polling places to all your people,

Allow men and women to register and vote whatever the color of their skin.

Extend the rights of citizenship to every citizen of this land.

There is no constitutional issue here. The command of the Constitution is plain.

There is no moral issue. It is wrong to deny any of our fellow Americans the right to vote.

There is no issue of states' rights or national rights. There is only the struggle for human rights.

I have not the slightest doubt what will be your answer.

The last time a President sent a civil rights bill to the Congress it contained a provision to protect voting rights in Federal elections. That civil rights bill was passed after eight long months of debate. And when that bill came to my desk from the Congress, the heart of the voting provision had been eliminated.

This time, on this issue, there must be no delay, no hesitation and no compromise with our purpose. . . .

What happened in Selma is part of a far larger movement which reaches into every section and state of America. It is the effort of American Negroes to secure for themselves the full blessings of American life.

Their cause must be our cause too. It is not just Negroes, but it is all of us, who must overcome the crippling legacy of bigotry and injustice.

And we shall overcome.

As a man whose roots go deeply into Southern soil I know how agonizing racial feelings are. I know how difficult it is to reshape the attitudes and the structure of our society.

But a century has passed, more than a hundred years, since the Negro was freed. And he is not fully free tonight.

It was more than a hundred years ago that Abraham Lincoln, a great President of the Republican party, signed the Emancipation Proclamation, but emancipation is a proclamation and not a fact.

A century has passed, more than a hundred years, since equality was promised. And yet the Negro is not equal.

A century has passed since the day of promise. And the promise is still unkept.

The time of justice has now come. I tell you I believe sincerely that no force can hold it back. It is right in the eyes of man and God that it should come. And when it does, I think that day will brighten the lives of every American.

For Negroes are not the only victims. How many white children have gone uneducated, how many white families have lived in stark poverty, how many white lives have been scarred by fear, because we wasted our energy and our substance to maintain the barriers of hatred and terror?

So I say to all of you here, and to all in the nation tonight, that those who appeal to you to hold on to the past do so at the cost of denying you your future.

This great, rich, restless country can offer opportunity and education and hope to all: black and white, North and South, sharecropper and city dweller. These are the enemies: poverty, ignorance, disease. They are the enemies and not our fellow man, not our neighbor. And these enemies too, poverty, disease, and ignorance, we shall overcome.

Let none of us look with prideful righteousness on the troubles in another section, or on the problems of our neighbors. There is no part of America where the promise of equality has been fully kept. In Buffalo as well as in Birmingham, in Philadelphia as well as in Selma, Americans are struggling for the fruits of freedom.

This is one nation. What happens in Selma or in Cincinnati is a matter of legitimate concern to every American. But let each of us look within our own hearts and our own communities, and let each of us put our shoulder to the wheel to root out injustice wherever it exists.

As we meet here in this historic chamber tonight, men from the South, some of whom were at Iwo Jima—men from the North who have carried Old Glory to far corners of the world and brought it back without a stain on it—men from the East and West, are all fighting together in Vietnam without regard to religion, or color, or region. Men from every region fought for us across the world twenty years ago. And in these common dangers and these common sacrifices the South made its contribution of honor and gallantry no less than any other region of the great Republic. And I have not the slightest doubt that good men from everywhere in this country, from the Great Lakes to the Gulf of Mexico, from the Golden Gate to the harbors along the Atlantic, will rally together now in this cause to vindicate the freedom of all Americans. For all of us owe his duty; and I believe all of us will respond to it.

Your President makes that request of every American.

The real hero of this struggle is the American Negro. His actions and protests, his courage to risk safety and even to risk his life, have awakened the conscience of this nation. His demonstrations have been designed to call attention to injustice, to provoke change, and to stir reform. He has called upon us to make good the promise of America. And who among us can say that we would have made the same progress were it not for his persistent bravery, and his faith in American democracy.

For at the real heart of battle for equality is a deep-seated belief in the democratic process. Equality depends not on the force of arms or tear gas but upon the force of moral right; not on recourse to violence but on respect for law and order.

There have been many pressures upon your President and there will be others as the days come and go. But I pledge you tonight that we intend to fight this battle where it should be fought: in the courts, and in Congress, and in the hearts of men.

We must preserve the right of free speech and the right of free assembly. But the right of free speech does not carry with it, as has been said, the right to holler fire in a crowded theater. We must preserve the right to free assembly, but free assembly does not carry with it the right to block public thoroughfares to traffic.

We do have a right to protest, and a right to march under conditions that do not infringe the Constitutional rights of our neighbors. And I intend to protect all those rights as long as I am permitted to serve in this office.

We will guard against violence, knowing it strikes from our hands the very weapons with which we seek progress—obedience to law and belief in American values.

In Selma as elsewhere we seek and pray for peace. We seek order. We seek unity. But we will not accept the peace of suppressed rights, or the order imposed by fear, or the unity that stifles protest. For peace cannot be purchased at the cost of liberty.

In Selma tonight, as in every city, we are working for just and peaceful settlement. We must all remember that after this speech I am making tonight, after the police and the FBI and the marshals have all gone, and after you have promptly passed this bill, the people of Selma and the other cities of the nation must still live and work together. And when the attention of the nation has gone elsewhere they must try to heal the wounds and to build a new community. This cannot be easily done on a battleground of violence, as the history of the South itself shows. It is in recognition of this that men of both races have shown such an outstandingly impressive responsibility in recent days.

The bill that I am presenting to you will be known as a civil rights bill. But, in a larger sense, most of the program I am recommending is a civil rights program. Its object is to open the city of hope to all people of all races.

All Americans must have the right to vote. And we are going to give them that right.

All Americans must have the privileges of citizenship regardless of race. And they are going to have those privileges of citizenship regardless of race.

But I would like to remind you that to exercise these privileges takes much more than just legal right. It requires a trained mind and a healthy body. It requires a decent home, and the chance to find a job, and the opportunity to escape from the clutches of poverty.

Of course, people cannot contribute to the nation if they are never taught to read or write, if their bodies are stunted from hunger, if their sickness goes untended, if their life is spent in hopeless poverty just drawing a welfare check.

So we want to open the gates to opportunity. But we are also going to give all our people, black and white, the help they need to walk through those gates.

QUESTIONS TO CONSIDER

1. What does President Johnson mean when he says that "emancipation is a proclamation and not a fact"?

2. What is the primary purpose of Johnson's speech?

3. Why do you think he repeats the phrase "we shall overcome" throughout his speech?

from

The Fire Next Time

BY JAMES BALDWIN

For more than a decade the Civil Rights movement seemed focused and unified in its nonviolent protests in the South. By the middle 1960s, some leaders challenged both the idea of integration and the use of nonviolent protest. New leaders like Malcolm X (see page 174) and Stokely Carmichael (see page 185) were rising up to challenge the course that had been set by men like Martin Luther King, Jr. and Thurgood Marshall. In his essay "The Fire Next Time," James Baldwin examined where African Americans stood in the United States in the 1960s. The first part, "My Dungeon Shook," took the form of a letter to Baldwin's nephew on the one-hundredth anniversary of the Emancipation Proclamation. The second part, "Down at the Cross," is a description of the forms of racism in the United States and a plea for unity.

White Americans find it as difficult as white people elsewhere do to **divest**[1] themselves of the notion that

---

[1] **divest**—to become free of; rid.

they are in possession of some intrinsic value that black people need, or want. And this assumption—which, for example, makes the solution to the Negro problem depend on the speed with which Negroes accept and adopt white standards—is revealed in all kinds of striking ways, from Bobby Kennedy's assurance that a Negro can become President in forty years to the unfortunate tone of warm congratulation with which so many liberals address their Negro equals. It is the Negro, of course, who is presumed to have become equal—an achievement that not only proves the comforting fact that perseverance has no color but also overwhelmingly **corroborates**[2] the white man's sense of his own value. Alas, this value can scarcely be corroborated in any other way; there is certainly little enough in the white man's public or private life that one should desire to imitate. White men, at the bottom of their hearts, know this. Therefore, a vast amount of the energy that goes into what we call the Negro problem is produced by the white man's profound desire not to be judged by those who are not white, not to be seen as he is, and at the same time a vast amount of the white anguish is rooted in the white man's equally profound need to be seen as he is, to be released from the tyranny of his mirror. All of us know, whether or not we are able to admit it, that mirrors can only lie, that death by drowning is all that awaits one there. It is for this reason that love is so desperately sought and so cunningly avoided. Love takes off the masks that we fear we cannot live without and know we cannot live within. I use the word "love" here not merely in the personal sense but as a state of being, or a state of grace—not in the infantile American sense of being made happy but in the tough and universal sense of quest and daring and growth. And I submit, then, that the racial tensions that menace

---

[2] **corroborates**—confirms; supports with evidence.

Americans today have little to do with real **antipathy**[3]—on the contrary, indeed—and are involved only symbolically with color. These tensions are rooted in the very same depths as those from which love springs, or murder. The white man's unadmitted—and apparently, to him, unspeakable—private fears and longings are projected onto the Negro. The only way he can be released from the Negro's tyrannical power over him is to consent, in effect, to become black himself, to become a part of that suffering and dancing country that he now watches wistfully from the heights of his lonely power and, armed with spiritual traveler's checks, visits **surreptitiously**[4] after dark. How can one respect, let alone adopt, the values of a people who do not, on any level whatever, live the way they say they do, or the way they say they should? I cannot accept the proposition that the four-hundred-year **travail**[5] of the American Negro should result merely in his attainment of the present level of the American civilization. I am far from convinced that being released from the African witch doctor was worthwhile if I am now—in order to support the moral contradictions and the spiritual **aridity**[6] of my life—expected to become dependent on the American psychiatrist. It is a bargain I refuse. The only thing white people have that black people need, or should want, is power—and no one holds power forever. White people cannot, in the generality, be taken as models of how to live. Rather, the white man is himself in sore need of new standards, which will release him from his confusion and place him once again in fruitful communion with the depths of his own being. And I repeat: The price of the liberation of the white people is the liberation of the blacks—the

---

[3] **antipathy**—a strong feeling of aversion or repugnance.

[4] **surreptitiously**—secretly; stealthily.

[5] **travail**—tribulation or agony; anguish.

[6] **aridity**—dullness; emptiness; dryness.

total liberation, in the cities, in the towns, before the law, and in the mind. . . .

In short, we, the black and the white, deeply need each other here if we are really to become a nation—if we are really, that is, to achieve our identity, our maturity, as men and women. To create one nation has proved to be a hideously difficult task; there is certainly no need now to create two, one black and one white. But white men with far more political power than that possessed by the Nation of Islam movement have been advocating exactly this, in effect, for generations. If this sentiment is honored when it falls from the lips of Senator Byrd,[7] then there is no reason it should not be honored when it falls from the lips of Malcolm X. And any Congressional committee wishing to investigate the latter must also be willing to investigate the former. They are expressing exactly the same sentiments and represent exactly the same danger. There is absolutely no reason to suppose that white people are better equipped to frame the laws by which I am to be governed than I am. It is entirely unacceptable that I should have no voice in the political affairs of my own country, for I am not a ward of America; I am one of the first Americans to arrive on these shores.

This past, the Negro's past . . . fear by day and night, fear as deep as the marrow of the bone; doubt that he was worthy of life, since everyone around him denied it; sorrow for his women, for his kinfolk, for his children, who needed his protection, and whom he could not protect; rage, hatred, and murder, hatred for white men so deep that it often turned against him and his own, and made all love, all trust, all joy impossible— this past, this endless struggle to achieve and reveal and confirm a human identity, human authority, yet

[7] Senator Byrd—refers to Robert C. Byrd (1917–), Senator from West Virginia famed for trying to block Civil Rights legislation.

contains, for all its horror, something very beautiful. I do not mean to be sentimental about suffering—enough is certainly as good as a feast—but people who cannot suffer can never grow up, can never discover who they are. That man who is forced each day to snatch his manhood, his identity, out of the fire of human cruelty that rages to destroy it knows, if he survives his effort, and even if he does not survive it, something about himself and human life that no school on earth—and, indeed, no church—can teach. He achieves his own authority, and that is unshakable. This is because, in order to save his life, he is forced to look beneath appearances, to take nothing for granted, to hear the meaning behind the words. If one is continually surviving the worst that life can bring, one eventually ceases to be controlled by a fear of what life can bring; whatever it brings must be borne. And at this level of experience one's bitterness begins to be **palatable,**[8] and hatred becomes too heavy a sack to carry. The apprehension of life here so briefly and inadequately sketched has been the experience of generations of Negroes, and it helps to explain how they have endured and how they have been able to produce children of kindergarten age who can walk through mobs to get to school. It demands great force and great cunning continually to assault the mighty and indifferent fortress of white supremacy, as Negroes in this country have done so long. It demands great spiritual resilience not to hate the hater whose foot is on your neck, and an even greater miracle of perception and charity not to teach your child to hate. The Negro boys and girls who are facing mobs today come out of a long line of improbable aristocrats—the only genuine aristocrats this country has produced. I say "this country" because their frame of reference was totally American.

---

[8] **palatable**—acceptable or agreeable.

They were **hewing**[9] out of the mountain of white supremacy the stone of their individuality. I have great respect for that unsung army of black men and women who trudged down back lanes and entered back doors, saying "Yes, sir" and "No, Ma'am" in order to acquire a new roof for the schoolhouse, new books, a new chemistry lab, more beds for the dormitories, more dormitories. They did not like saying "Yes, sir" and "No Ma'am," but the country was in a hurry to educate Negroes, these black men and women knew that the job had to be done, and they put their pride in their pockets in order to do it. It is very hard to believe that they were in any way inferior to the white men and women who opened those back doors. It is very hard to believe that those men and women, raising their children, eating their greens, crying their curses, weeping their tears, singing their songs . . . as the sun rose, as the sun set, were in any way inferior to the white men and women who crept over to share these splendors after the sun went down. But we must avoid the European error; we must not suppose that, because the situation, the ways, the perceptions of black people so radically differed from those of whites, they were racially superior. I am proud of these people not because of their color but because of their intelligence and their spiritual force and their beauty. The country should be proud of them, too, but, alas, not many people in this country even know of their existence. And the reason for this ignorance is that a knowledge of the role these people played—and play—in American life would reveal more about America to Americans than Americans wish to know.

The American Negro has the great advantage of having never believed that collection of myths to which white Americans cling: that their ancestors were all

---

[9] **hewing**—cutting.

freedom-loving heroes, that they were born in the greatest country the world has ever seen, or that Americans are invincible in battle and wise in peace, that Americans have always dealt honorably with Mexicans and Indians and all other neighbors or inferiors, that American men are the world's most direct and virile, that American women are pure. Negroes know far more about white Americans than that; it can almost be said, in fact, that they know about white Americans what parents—or, anyway, mothers—know about their children, and that they very often regard white Americans that way. And perhaps this attitude, held in spite of what they know and have endured, helps to explain why Negroes, on the whole, and until lately, have allowed themselves to feel so little hatred. The tendency has really been, insofar as this was possible, to dismiss white people as the slightly mad victims of their own brainwashing. One watched the lives they led. One could not be fooled about that; one watched the things they did and the excuses that they gave themselves, and if a white man was really in trouble, deep trouble, it was to the Negro's door that he came. And one felt that if one had had that white man's worldly advantages, one would never have become as bewildered and as joyless and as thoughtlessly cruel as he. And the Negro knew this, too. When one knows this about a man, it is impossible for one to hate him, but unless he becomes a man—becomes equal—it is also impossible for one to love him. Ultimately, one tends to avoid him, for the universal characteristic of children is to assume that they have a monopoly on trouble, and therefore a monopoly on *you*. (Ask any Negro what he knows about the white people with whom he works. And then ask the white people with whom he works what they know about *him*.)

How can the American Negro past be used? It is entirely possible that this dishonored past will rise up soon to **smite**[10] all of us. There are some wars, for example (if anyone on the globe is still mad enough to go to war), that the American Negro will not support, however many of his people may be coerced—and there is a limit to the number of people any government can put in prison, and a rigid limit indeed to the practicality of such a course. A bill is coming in that I fear America is not prepared to pay. "The problem of the twentieth century," wrote W. E. B. Du Bois[11] around sixty years ago, "is the problem of the color line." A fearful and delicate problem, which compromises, when it does not corrupt, all the American efforts to build a better world—here, there, or anywhere. It is for this reason that everything white Americans think they believe in must now be reexamined. What one would not like to see again is the consolidation of peoples on the basis of their color. But as long as we in the West place on color the value that we do, we make it impossible for the great unwashed to consolidate themselves according to any other principle. Color is not a human or a personal reality; it is a political reality. But this is a distinction so extremely hard to make that the West has not been able to make it yet. And at the center of this dreadful storm, this vast confusion, stand the black people of this nation, who must now share the fate of a nation that has never accepted them, to which they were brought in chains. Well, if this is so, one has no choice but to do all in one's power to change that fate, and at no matter what risk—eviction, imprisonment, torture, death. For the sake of one's children, in order to minimize the bill that *they* must pay, one must be careful not to take refuge in any delusion—and the value placed on the color of the skin is always and

---

[10] **smite**—attack, damage, or destroy.

[11] W. E. B. Du Bois (1868–1963)—African-American writer and educator.

everywhere and forever a delusion. I know that what I am asking is impossible. But in our time, as in every time, the impossible is the least that one can demand—and one is, after all, emboldened by the spectacle of human history in general, and American Negro history in particular, for it testifies to nothing less than the perpetual achievement of the impossible.

When I was very young, and was dealing with my buddies, . . . something in me wondered, *What will happen to all that beauty?* For black people, though I am aware that some of us, black and white, do not know it yet, are very beautiful. And when I sat at Elijah's table and watched the baby, the women, and the men, and we talked about God's—or Allah's—vengeance, I wondered, when that vengeance was achieved, *What will happen to all that beauty then?* I could also see that the **intransigence**[12] and ignorance of the white world might make that vengeance inevitable—a vengeance that does not really depend on, and cannot really be executed by, any person or organization, and that cannot be prevented by any police force or army: historical vengeance, a cosmic vengeance, based on the law that we recognize when we say, "Whatever goes up must come down." And here we are, at the center of the arc, trapped in the gaudiest, most valuable, and most improbable water wheel the world has ever seen. Everything now, we must assume, is in our hands; we have no right to assume otherwise. If we—and now I mean the relatively conscious whites and the relatively conscious blacks, who must, like lovers, insist on, or create, the consciousness of the others—do not falter in our duty now, we may be able, handful that we are, to end the racial nightmare, and achieve

---

[12] **intransigence**—refusal to moderate a position, especially an extreme position.

our country, and change the history of the world. If we do not now dare everything, the fulfillment of that prophecy, re-created from the Bible in song by a slave, is upon us: *God gave Noah the rainbow sign, No more water, the fire next time!*

QUESTIONS TO CONSIDER

1. What does Baldwin want for African Americans?

2. Does Baldwin believe that violence between blacks and whites is inevitable? Explain.

3. How does the biblical reference to Noah ("God gave Noah the rainbow sign, No more water, the fire next time!") apply to Baldwin's call to "end the racial nightmare"?

Tragedy and Triumph

▲
From Little Acorns? Cartoon by Edward
Marcus depicts how the Civil Rights Act of
1964 could change the nation.

◄ **Marching** Martin Luther King, Jr., speaks to protest
marchers while the motto of the movement is held up.

▲

UHURU! African-American protesters march. *Uhuru* is a slogan in Swahili that means "freedom."

Trying to Register African Americans line up
to try to register to vote, while a white man is
allowed through.
▼

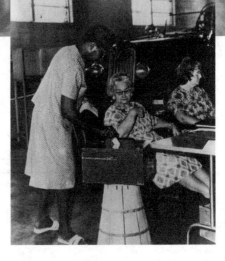

▲
Backlash Police dogs attack a
protester in Mississippi.

Voting An African-American woman
uses her hard-won right to cast a
vote in the 1966 congressional election
in Mississippi. ▶

New Voices
and Ideas

"The Black Revolution"

BY MALCOLM X

As the former colonies in Africa became independent nations in the 1960s, many African Americans began to look to Africa for inspiration. They identified their struggle for racial equality with the African's long struggle for independence. For various African-American groups this identification took the form of advocating separatism rather than integration. The most famous of these groups was the Nation of Islam, also known as the Black Muslims. Led by Elijah Muhammad, the Black Muslims advocated absolute racial separation, calling on African Americans to develop self-reliance and independence. One of the movement's most eloquent spokesmen was Malcolm X (1925–1965). In 1964 Malcolm X broke with the Nation of Islam over its hardline anti-white bias. The following is an excerpt from a speech Malcolm X gave in New York in 1964, not long after his break with Elijah Muhammad. Malcolm X was assassinated in 1965 by estranged members of the Black Muslims.

Friends and enemies: Tonight I hope that we can have a little fireside chat with as few sparks as possible being tossed around. Especially because of the very explosive condition that the world is in today. Sometimes, when a person's house is on fire and someone comes in yelling fire, instead of the person who is awakened by the yell being thankful, he makes the mistake of charging the one who awakened him with having set the fire. I hope that this little conversation tonight about the black revolution won't cause many of you to accuse us of igniting it when you find it at your doorstep. . . .

Any kind of racial explosion that takes place in this country today, in 1964, is not a racial explosion that can be confined to the shores of America. It is a racial explosion that can ignite the racial powder keg that exists all over the planet that we call earth. I think that nobody would disagree that the dark masses of Africa and Asia and Latin America are already seething with bitterness, animosity, hostility, unrest, and impatience with the racial intolerance that they themselves have experienced at the hands of the white West.

And just as they have the ingredients of hostility toward the West in general, here we also have 22 million African Americans, black, brown, red, and yellow people, in this country who are also seething with bitterness and impatience and hostility and animosity at the racial intolerance not only of the white West but of white America in particular.

And by the hundreds of thousands today we find our own people have become impatient, turning away from your white nationalism, which you call democracy, toward the militant, uncompromising policy of black nationalism. I point out right here that as soon as we announced we were going to start a black nationalist party in this country, we received mail from coast to coast, especially from young people at the college level, the university level, who expressed complete sympathy and support and a desire to take an active part in any kind of political action based on black nationalism, designed to correct or eliminate immediately evils that our people have suffered here for 400 years.

The black nationalists to many of you may represent only a minority in the community. And therefore you might have a tendency to classify them as something insignificant. But just as the fuse is the smallest part or the smallest piece in the powder keg, it is yet that little fuse that ignites the entire powder keg. The black nationalists to you may represent a small minority in the so-called Negro community. But they just happen to be composed of the type of ingredient necessary to fuse or ignite the entire black community.

And this is one thing that whites—whether you call yourselves liberals or conservatives or racists or whatever else you might choose to be—one thing that you have to realize is, where the black community is concerned, although the large majority you come in contact with may impress you as being moderate and patient and loving and long-suffering and all that kind of stuff, the minority who you consider to be Muslims or nationalists happen to be made of the type of ingredient that can easily spark the black community. This should be understood. Because to me a powder keg is nothing without a fuse.

1964 will be America's hottest year; her hottest year yet; a year of much racial violence and much racial bloodshed. But it won't be blood that's going to flow only on one side. The new generation of black people that have grown up in this country during recent years are already forming the opinion, and it's a just opinion, that if there is to be bleeding, it should be reciprocal— bleeding on both sides.

It should also be understood that the racial sparks that are ignited here in America today could easily turn into a flaming fire abroad, which means it could engulf all the people of this earth into a giant race war. You cannot confine it to one little neighborhood, or one little community, or one little country. What happens to a black man in America today happens to the black man in Africa. What happens to a black man in America and Africa happens to the black man in Asia and to the man down in Latin America. What happens to one of us today happens to all of us. And when this is realized, I think that the whites—who are intelligent even if they aren't moral or aren't just or aren't impressed by legalities—those who are intelligent will realize that when they touch this one, they are touching all of them, and this in itself will have a tendency to be a checking factor.

The seriousness of this situation must be faced up to. I was in Cleveland last night, Cleveland, Ohio. In fact I was there Friday, Saturday and yesterday. Last Friday the warning was given that this is a year of bloodshed, that the black man has ceased to turn the other cheek, that he has ceased to be nonviolent, that he has ceased to feel that he must be confined by all these restraints that are put upon him by white society in struggling for what white society says he was supposed to have had a hundred years ago.

So today, when the black man starts reaching out for what America says are his rights, the black man feels that he is within his rights—when he becomes the victim of brutality by those who are depriving him of his rights—to do whatever is necessary to protect himself. An example of this was taking place last night at this same time in Cleveland, where the police were putting water hoses on our people there and also throwing tear gas at them—and they met a hail of stones, a hail of rocks, a hail of bricks. A couple of weeks ago in Jacksonville, Florida, a young teen-age Negro was throwing Molotov cocktails.[1]

---

[1] Molotov cocktails—crude homemade bombs.

Well, Negroes didn't do this ten years ago. But what you should learn from this is that they are waking up. It was stones yesterday, Molotov cocktails today; it will be hand grenades tomorrow and whatever else is available the next day. The seriousness of this situation must be faced up to. You should not feel that I am inciting someone to violence. I'm only warning of a powder-keg situation. You can take it or leave it. If you take the warning, perhaps you can still save yourself. But if you ignore it or ridicule it, well, death is already at your doorstep. There are 22 million African Americans who are ready to fight for independence right here. When I say fight for independence right here, I don't mean any nonviolent fight, or turn-the-other-cheek fight. Those days are gone. Those days are over.

If George Washington didn't get independence for this country nonviolently, and if Patrick Henry didn't come up with a nonviolent statement, and you taught me to look upon them as patriots and heroes, then it's time for you to realize that I have studied your books well. . . .

1964 will see the Negro revolt evolve and merge into the world-wide black revolution that has been taking place on this earth since 1945. The so-called revolt will become a real black revolution. Now the black revolution has been taking place in Africa and Asia and Latin America; when I say black, I mean non-white—black, brown, red or yellow. Our brothers and sisters in Asia, who were colonized by the Europeans, our brothers and sisters in Africa, who were colonized by the Europeans, and in Latin America, the peasants, who were colonized by the Europeans, have been involved in a struggle since 1945 to get the colonialists, or the colonizing powers, the Europeans, off their land, out of their country.

This is a real revolution. Revolution is always based on land. Revolution is never based on begging somebody for an integrated cup of coffee. Revolutions are never fought by turning the other cheek. Revolutions are never based upon love-your-enemy and pray-for-those-who-spitefully-use-you. And revolutions are never waged singing "We Shall Overcome." Revolutions are based upon bloodshed. Revolutions are never compromising. Revolutions are never based upon negotiations. Revolutions are never based upon any kind of tokenism[2] whatsoever. Revolutions are never even based upon that which is begging a corrupt society or a corrupt system to accept us into it. Revolutions overturn systems. And there is no system on this earth which has proven itself more corrupt, more criminal, than this system that in 1964 still colonizes 22 million African Americans, still enslaves 22 million Afro-Americans.

There is no system more corrupt than a system that represents itself as the example of freedom, the example of democracy, and can go all over this earth telling other people how to straighten out their house, when you have citizens of this country who have to use bullets if they want to cast a ballot.

The greatest weapon the colonial powers have used in the past against our people has always been divide-and-conquer. America is a colonial power. She has colonized 22 million Afro-Americans by depriving us of first-class citizenship, by depriving us of civil rights, actually by depriving us of human rights. She has not only deprived us of the right to be a citizen, she has deprived us of the right to be human beings, the right to be recognized and respected as men and women. In this country the black can be fifty years old and he is still a "boy."

I grew up with white people. I was integrated before they even invented the word and I have never met white people yet—if you are around them long enough—who won't refer to you as a "boy" or a "gal," no matter how

---

[2] tokenism—the policy of making only a token effort.

old you are or what school you came out of, no matter what your intellectual or professional level is. In this society we remain "boys."

So America's strategy is the same strategy as that which was used in the past by the colonial powers: divide and conquer. She plays one Negro leader against the other. She plays one Negro organization against the other. She makes us think we have different objectives, different goals. As soon as one Negro says something, she runs to this Negro and asks him, "What do you think about what he said?" Why, anybody can see through that today—except some of the Negro leaders.

All of our people have the same goals, the same objective. That objective is freedom, justice, equality. All of us want recognition and respect as human beings. We don't want to be integrationists. Nor do we want to be separationists. We want to be human beings. Integration is only a method that is used by some groups to obtain freedom, justice, equality and respect as human beings. Separation is only a method that is used by other groups to obtain freedom, justice, equality or human dignity.

Our people have made the mistake of confusing the methods with the objectives. As long as we agree on objectives, we should never fall out with each other just because we believe in different methods or tactics or strategy to reach a common objective.

We have to keep in mind at all times that we are not fighting for integration, nor are we fighting for separation. We are fighting for recognition as human beings. We are fighting for the right to live as free humans in this society. In fact, we are actually fighting for rights that are even greater than civil rights and that is human rights.

Among the so-called Negroes in this country, as a rule the civil-rights groups, those who believe in civil rights, spend most of their time trying to prove they are Americans. Their thinking is usually domestic, confined to the boundaries of America, and they always look upon themselves as a minority. When they look upon themselves upon the American stage, the American stage is a white stage. So a black man standing on that stage in America automatically is in the minority. He is the underdog, and in his struggle he always uses an approach that is a begging, hat-in-hand, compromising approach.

Whereas the other segment or section in America, known as the black nationalists, are more interested in human rights than they are in civil rights. And they place more stress on human rights than they do on civil rights. The difference between the thinking and the scope of the Negroes who are involved in the human-rights struggle and those who are involved in the civil-rights struggle is that those so-called Negroes involved in the human-rights struggle don't look upon themselves as Americans.

They look upon themselves as a part of dark mankind. They see the whole struggle not within the confines of the American stage, but they look upon the struggle on the world stage. And, in the world context, they see that the dark man outnumbers the white man. On the world stage the white man is just a microscopic minority.

So in this country you find two different types of Afro-Americans—the type who looks upon himself as a minority and you as the majority, because his scope is limited to the American scene; and then you have the type who looks upon himself as part of the majority and you as part of a microscopic minority. And this one uses a different approach in trying to struggle for his rights. He doesn't beg. He doesn't thank you for what you give him, because you are only giving him what he should have had a hundred years ago. He doesn't think you are doing him any favors.

He doesn't see any progress that he has made since the Civil War. He sees not one iota of progress because, number one, if the Civil War had freed him, he wouldn't need civil-rights legislation today. If the Emancipation Proclamation, issued by that great shining liberal called Lincoln, had freed him, he wouldn't be singing "We Shall Overcome" today. If the amendments to the Constitution had solved his problem, his problem wouldn't still be here today. And if the Supreme Court desegregation decision of 1954 was genuinely and sincerely designed to solve his problem, his problem wouldn't be with us today.

So this kind of black man is thinking. He can see where every maneuver that America has made, supposedly to solve this problem, has been nothing but political trickery and treachery of the worst order. Today he doesn't have any confidence in these so-called liberals. (I know that all that have come in here tonight don't call yourselves liberals. Because that's a nasty name today. It represents hypocrisy.) So these two different types of black people exist in the so-called Negro community and they are beginning to wake up and their awakening is producing a very dangerous situation.

So, in my conclusion, in speaking about the black revolution, America today is at a time or in a day or at an hour where she is the first country on this earth that can actually have a bloodless revolution. In the past, revolutions have been bloody. Historically you just don't have a peaceful revolution. Revolutions are bloody, revolutions are violent, revolutions cause bloodshed and death follows in their paths. America is the only country in history in a position to bring about a revolution without violence and bloodshed. But America is not morally equipped to do so.

Why is America in a position to bring about a bloodless revolution? Because the Negro in this country holds the balance of power, and if the Negro in this country were given what the Constitution says he is supposed to have, the added power of the Negro in this country would sweep all of the racists and the segregationists out of office. It would change the entire political structure of the country. It would wipe out the Southern segregationism that now controls America's foreign policy, as well as America's domestic policy.

And the only way without bloodshed that this can be brought about is that the black man has to be given full use of the ballot in every one of the fifty states. But if the black man doesn't get the ballot, then you are going to be faced with another man who forgets the ballot and starts using the bullet.

Revolutions are fought to get control of land, to remove the absentee landlord and gain control of the land and the institutions that flow from that land. The black man has been in a very low condition because he has had no control whatsoever over any land. He has been a beggar economically, a beggar politically, a beggar socially, a beggar even when it comes to trying to get some education. The past type of mentality, that was developed in this colonial system among our people, today is being overcome. And as the young ones come up, they know what they want. And as they listen to your beautiful preaching about democracy and all those other flowery words, they know what they're supposed to have.

So you have a people today who not only know what they want, but also know what they are supposed to have. And they themselves are creating another generation that is coming up that not only will know what it wants and know what it should have, but also will be ready and willing to do whatever is necessary to see that what they should have materializes immediately. Thank you.

QUESTIONS TO CONSIDER

1. What does Malcolm X mean when he says that there is a "powder-keg situation" in the African-American community?

2. According to Malcolm X, what is the difference between the goals of integrationists and the goals of separationists?

3. What distinction does Malcolm X make between those fighting for civil rights and those fighting for human rights?

What We Want

BY STOKELY CARMICHAEL

While nonviolence had once been the hallmark of the Civil Rights movement and its leadership, by 1965, new leaders and new protesters were employing more militant methods. The Watts Riots in Los Angeles in August 1965 and riots in other large cities made it clear that there were a number of African Americans who felt excluded from American society and who were seething with rage. Stokely Carmichael, the leader of SNCC, coined a term for this underlying tension: Black Power. He said, "Integration is irrelevant. Political and economic power is what the black people have to have." Carmichael transformed SNCC from an interracial organization that promoted nonviolence and integration to an all African American one that supported violence and separatism. The following selection is from an essay Carmichael wrote in 1966 for The New York Review of Books *in which he tries to define "Black Power."*

One of the tragedies of the struggle against racism is that up to now there has been no national organization that could speak to the growing militancy of young black people in the urban ghetto. There has been only a civil rights movement, whose tone of voice was adapted to an audience of liberal whites. It served as a sort of buffer zone between them and angry young blacks. None of its so-called leaders could go into a rioting community and be listened to. In a sense, I blame ourselves—together with the mass media—for what has happened in Watts, Harlem, Chicago, Cleveland, and Omaha. Each time the people in those cities saw Martin Luther King get slapped, they became angry; when they saw four little black girls bombed to death, they were angrier; and when nothing happened, they were steaming. We had nothing to offer that they could see, except to go out and be beaten again. We helped to build their frustration.

For too many years, black Americans marched and had their heads broken and got shot. They were saying to the country, "Look, you guys are supposed to be nice guys and we are only going to do what we are supposed to do—why do you beat us up, why don't you give us what we ask, why don't you straighten yourself out?" After years of this, we are at almost the same point— because we demonstrated from a position of weakness. We cannot be expected any longer to march and have our heads broken in order to say to whites: Come on, you're nice guys. For you are not nice guys. We have found you out.

An organization which claims to speak for the needs of a community—as does the Student Nonviolent Coordinating Committee—must speak in the tone of that community, not as somebody else's buffer zone. This is the significance of Black Power as a slogan. For once, black people are going to use the words they want to use—not just the words whites want to hear. And they will do this no matter how often the press tries to stop the use of the slogan by equating it with racism or separatism.

An organization which claims to be working for the needs of a community—as SNCC does—must work to provide that community with a position of strength from which to make its voice heard. This is the significance of Black Power beyond the slogan.

Black Power can be clearly defined for those who do not attach the fears of white America to their questions about it. We should begin with the basic fact that black Americans have two problems: they are poor and they are black. All other problems arise from this two-sided reality: lack of education, the so-called apathy of black men. Any program to end racism must address itself to that double reality.

Almost from its beginning, SNCC sought to address itself to both conditions with a program aimed at winning political power for impoverished Southern blacks. We had to begin with politics because black Americans are a propertyless people in a country where property is valued above all. We had to work for power, because this country does not function by morality, love, and nonviolence, but by power. Thus we determined to win political power, with the idea of moving on from there into activity that would have economic effects. With power, the masses could make or participate in making the decisions which govern their destinies, and thus create basic change in their day-to-day lives. . . .

Politically, Black Power means what it has always meant to SNCC: the coming-together of black people to elect representatives and *to force those representatives to speak to their needs.* It does not mean merely putting black faces into office. A man or woman who is black and from the slums cannot be automatically expected to speak to the needs of black people. Most of the black politicians we see around the country today are not what SNCC means by Black Power. The power must be that of a community, and emanate from there.

SNCC today is working in both North and South on programs of voter registration and independent political organizing. In some places, such as Alabama, Los Angeles, New York, Philadelphia, and New Jersey, independent organizing under the black panther symbol is in progress. The creation of a national "black panther party" must come about; it will take time to build, and it is much too early to predict its success. We have no infallible master plan and we make no claim to exclusive knowledge of how to end racism; different groups will work in their own different ways. SNCC cannot spell out the full logistics of self-determination, but it can address itself to the problem by helping black communities define their needs, realize their strength, and go into action along a variety of lines which they must choose for themselves. Without knowing all the answers, it can address itself to the basic problem of poverty, to the fact that in Lowndes County 86 white families own 90 percent of the land. What are black people in that county going to do for jobs; where are they going to get money? There must be reallocation of land, of money. . . .

To most whites, Black Power seems to mean that the Mau Mau[1] are coming to the suburbs at night. The Mau Mau are coming, and whites must stop them. Articles appear about plots to "get Whitey," creating an atmosphere in which "law and order must be maintained." Once again, responsibility is shifted from the oppressor to the oppressed. Other whites chide, "Don't forget— you're only 10 percent of the population; if you get too smart, we'll wipe you out." If they are liberals, they complain, "What about me—don't you want my help any more?" These are people supposedly concerned

---

[1] Mau Mau—militant African Nationalist movement that originated in the 1950s among the Kikuku people of Kenya.

about black Americans, but today they think first of themselves, of their feelings of rejection. Or they admonish, "You can't get anywhere without coalitions," when there is in fact no group at present with whom to form a coalition in which blacks will not be absorbed and betrayed. Or they accuse us of "polarizing the races" by our calls for black unity, when the true responsibility for polarization lies with whites who will not accept their responsibility as the majority power for making the democratic process work.

White America will not face the problem of color, the reality of it. The well-intended say: "We're all human, everybody is really decent, we must forget color." But color cannot be "forgotten" until its weight is recognized and dealt with. White America will not acknowledge that the ways in which this country sees itself are contradicted by being black—and always have been. Whereas most of the people who settled this country came here for freedom or for economic opportunity, blacks were brought here to be slaves. When the Lowndes County Freedom Organization chose the black panther as its symbol, it was christened by the press "the Black Panther Party"—but the Alabama Democratic Party, whose symbol is a rooster, has never been called the White Cock Party. No one ever talked about "white power" because power in this country is white. All this adds up to more than merely identifying a group phenomenon by some catchy name or adjective. The furor over that black panther reveals the problems that white America has with color and sex; the furor over Black Power reveals how deep racism runs and the great fear which is attached to it.

Whites will not see that I, for example, as a person oppressed because of my blackness, have common cause with other blacks who are oppressed because of blackness. This is not to say that there are no white people who see things as I do, but that it is black people I must speak to first. It must be the oppressed to whom SNCC addresses itself primarily, not to friends from the oppressing group.

From birth, black people are told a set of lies about themselves. We are told that we are lazy—yet I drive through the Delta area of Mississippi and watch black people picking cotton in the hot sun for fourteen hours. We are told, "If you work hard, you'll succeed"—but if that were true, black people would own this country. We are oppressed because we are black—not because we are ignorant, not because we are lazy, not because we're stupid (and got good rhythm), but because we're black.

I remember that when I was a boy I used to go to see Tarzan movies on Saturday. White Tarzan used to beat up the black natives. I would sit there yelling, "Kill the beasts, kill the savages, kill 'em!" I was saying: Kill me. It was as if a Jewish boy watched Nazis taking Jews off to concentration camps and cheered them on. Today, I want the chief to beat hell out of Tarzan and send him back to Europe. But it takes time to become free of the lies and their shaming effect on black minds. It takes time to reject the most important lie: that black people inherently can't do the same things white people can do, unless white people help them.

The need for psychological equality is the reason why SNCC today believes that blacks must organize in the black community. Only black people can convey the revolutionary idea that black people are able to do things themselves. Only they can help create in the community an aroused and continuing black consciousness that will provide the basis for political strength. In the past, white allies have furthered white supremacy without the whites involved realizing it—or wanting it, I think. Black people must do things for themselves; they must get poverty money they will control and spend themselves, they must conduct tutorial programs themselves so that black children can identify with black people. This is one reason Africa has such importance: the reality of black men ruling their own nations gives blacks elsewhere a sense of possibility, of power, which they do not now have. . . .

Black people do not want to "take over" this country. They don't want to "get Whitey"; they just want to get him off their backs, as the saying goes. . . . The white man is irrelevant to blacks, except as an oppressive force. Blacks want to be in his place, yes, but not in order to terrorize and lynch and starve him. They want to be in his place because that is where a decent life can be had.

But our vision is not merely of a society in which all black men have enough to buy the good things of life. When we urge that black money go into black pockets, we mean the communal pocket. We want to see money go back into the community and used to benefit it. We want to see the cooperative concept applied in business and banking. We want to see black ghetto residents demand that an exploiting landlord or storekeeper sell them, at minimal cost, a building or a shop that they will own and improve cooperatively; they can back their demand with a rent strike, or a boycott, and a community so unified behind them that no one else will move into the building or buy at the store. The society we seek to build among black people, then, is not a capitalist one. It is a society in which the spirit of community and humanistic love prevail. The word "love" is suspect; black expectations of what it might produce have been betrayed too often. But those were expectations of a response from the white community, which failed us. The love we seek to encourage is within the black community, the only American community where men call each other "brother" when they meet. We can build a community of love only where we have the ability and power to do so: among blacks.

As for white America, perhaps it can stop crying out against "black supremacy," "black nationalism," "racism in reverse," and begin facing reality. The reality is that this nation is racist; that racism is not primarily a problem of "human relations" but of an exploitation maintained—either actively or through silence—by the society as a whole. Can whites, particularly liberal whites, condemn themselves? Can they stop blaming us, and blame their own system? Are they capable of the shame which might become a revolutionary emotion?

We have found that they usually cannot condemn themselves, and so we have done it. But the rebuilding of this society, if at all possible, is basically the responsibility of whites—not blacks. We won't fight to save the present society, in Vietnam or anywhere else. We are just going to work, in the way we see fit, and on goals we define, not for civil rights but for all our human rights.

QUESTIONS TO CONSIDER

1. What does Stokely Carmichael say are the weaknesses of the nonviolence movement?

2. Why are many whites frightened by the whole notion of Black Power?

3. What are some of the lies that black people have been told about themselves?

4. According to Carmichael, what do African Americans want?

The Civil Rights Movement: What Good Was It?

BY ALICE WALKER

Alice Walker was born in 1944 in Eatonville, Georgia, into a family of sharecroppers. Walker grew up in poverty, but thanks to a scholarship was able to go to college in 1961 where she discovered the Civil Rights movement. She participated in demonstrations and discovered the power of protest. Walker deeply admired the courageous and dedicated leaders of the movement. Shortly after graduation in 1965, Walker moved to Mississippi and worked on the voter registration campaigns. She also spent time collecting folklore and stories from African-American women in Mississippi. In 1966, Walker wrote the following essay describing the movement and what it meant to her.

Someone said recently to an old black lady from Mississippi, whose legs had been badly mangled by local police who arrested her for "disturbing the peace," that the Civil Rights Movement was dead, and asked, since it was dead, what she thought about it. The old lady replied, hobbling out of his presence on her cane, that the Civil Rights Movement was like herself, "if it's dead, it shore ain't ready to lay down!"

This old lady is a legendary freedom fighter in her small town in the Delta. She has been severely mistreated for insisting on her rights as an American citizen. She has been beaten for singing Movement songs, placed in solitary confinement in prisons for talking about freedom, and placed on bread and water for praying aloud to God for her jailers' deliverance. For such a woman the Civil Rights Movement will never be over as long as her skin is black. It also will never be over for twenty million others with the same "affliction," for whom the Movement can never "lay down," no matter how it is killed by the press and made dead and buried by the white American public. As long as one black American survives, the struggle for equality with other Americans must also survive. This is a debt we owe to those blameless hostages we leave to the future, our children.

Still, white liberals and deserting Civil Rights sponsors are quick to justify their disaffection from the Movement by claiming that it is all over. "And since it is over," they will ask, "would someone kindly tell me what has been gained by it?" They then list statistics supposedly showing how much more advanced segregation is now than ten years ago—in schools, housing, jobs. They point to a gain in conservative politicians during the last few years. They speak of ghetto riots and of the survey that shows that most policemen are admittedly too anti-Negro to do their jobs in ghetto areas fairly and effectively. They speak of every area that has been touched by the Civil Rights Movement as somehow or other going to pieces.

They rarely talk, however, about human attitudes among Negroes that have undergone terrific changes just during the past seven to ten years (not to mention all those years when there was a Movement and only the Negroes knew about it). They seldom speak of changes in personal lives because of the influence of people in the Movement. They see general failure and few, if any, individual gains.

They do not understand what it is that keeps the Movement from "laying down" and Negroes from reverting to their former silent second-class status. They have apparently never stopped to wonder why it is always the white man—on his radio and in his newspaper and on his television—who says that the Movement is dead. If a Negro were **audacious**[1] enough to make such a claim, his fellows might **hanker**[2] to see him shot. The Movement is dead to the white man because it no longer interests him. And it no longer interests him because he can afford to be uninterested: he does not have to live by it, with it, or for it, as Negroes must. He can take a rest from the news of beatings, killings, and arrests that reach him from North and South—if his skin is white. Negroes cannot now and will never be able to take a rest from the injustices that plague them, for they—not the white man—are the target.

Perhaps it is naïve to be thankful that the Movement "saved" a large number of individuals and gave them something to live for, even if it did not provide them with everything they wanted. (Materially, it provided them with precious little that they wanted.) When a movement awakens people to the possibilities of life, it seems unfair to frustrate them by then denying what they had thought was offered. But what was offered?

[1] **audacious**—daring, bold.

[2] **hanker**—yearn.

What was promised? What was it all about? What good did it do? Would it have been better, as some have suggested, to leave the Negro people as they were, unawakened, unallied with one another, unhopeful about what to expect for their children in some future world?

I do not think so. If knowledge of my condition is all the freedom I get from a "freedom movement," it is better than unawareness, forgottenness, and hopelessness, the existence that is like the existence of a beast. Man only truly lives by knowing; otherwise he simply performs, copying the daily habits of others, but conceiving nothing of his creative possibilities as a man, and accepting someone else's superiority and his own misery.

When we are children, growing up in our parents' care, we await the spark from the outside world. Sometimes our parents provide it—if we are lucky—sometimes it comes from another source far from home. We sit, paralyzed, surrounded by our anxiety and dread, hoping we will not have to grow up into the narrow world and ways we see about us. We are hungry for a life that turns us on; we yearn for a knowledge of living that will save us from our **innocuous**[3] lives that resemble death. We look for signs in every strange event; we search for heroes in every unknown face.

It was just six years ago that I began to be alive. I had, of course, been living before—for I am now twenty-three—but I did not really know it. And I did not know it because nobody told me that I—a pensive, yearning, typical high-school senior, but Negro—existed in the minds of others as I existed in my own. Until that time my mind was locked apart from the outer contours and complexion of my body as if it and the body were strangers. The mind possessed both thought and

---

[3] **innocuous**—inoffensive; not arousing strong feelings.

spirit—I wanted to be an author or a scientist—which the color of the body denied. I had never seen myself and existed as a statistic exists, or as a phantom. In the white world I walked, less real to them than a shadow; and being young and well hidden among the slums, among people who also did not exist—either in books or in films or in the government of their own lives—I waited to be called to life. And, by a miracle, I was called. . . .

The Civil Rights Movement came into my life. Like a good omen for the future, the face of Dr. Martin Luther King, Jr., was the first black face I saw on our new television screen. And, as in a fairy tale, my soul was stirred by the meaning for me of his mission—at the time he was being rather **ignominiously**[4] dumped into a police van for having led a protest march in Alabama—and I fell in love with the sober and determined face of the Movement. The singing of "We Shall Overcome"—that song betrayed by nonbelievers in it—rang for the first time in my ears. The influence that my mother's soap operas might have had on me became impossible. The life of Dr. King, seeming bigger and more miraculous than the man himself, because of all he had done and suffered, offered a pattern of strength and sincerity I felt I could trust. He had suffered much because of his simple belief in nonviolence, love, and brotherhood. Perhaps the majority of men could not be reached through these beliefs, but because Dr. King kept trying to reach them in spite of danger to himself and his family, I saw in him the hero for whom I had waited so long.

What Dr. King promised was not a ranch-style house and an acre of manicured lawn for every black man, but jail and finally freedom. He did not promise two cars for every family, but the courage one day for all

[4] **ignominiously**—shamefully.

families everywhere to walk without shame and unafraid on their own feet. He did not say that one day it will be us chasing prospective buyers out of our prosperous well-kept neighborhoods, or in other ways exhibiting our snobbery and ignorance as all other ethnic groups before us have done; what he said was that we had a right to live anywhere in this country we chose, and a right to a meaningful well-paying job to provide us with the upkeep of our homes. He did not say we had to become carbon copies of the white American middle class; but he did say we had the right to become whatever we wanted to become.

Because of the Movement, because of an awakened faith in the newness and imagination of the human spirit, because of "black and white together"—for the first time in our history in some human relationship on and off TV—because of the beatings, the arrests, the hell of battle during the past years, I have fought harder for my life and for a chance to be myself, to be something more than a shadow or a number, than I had ever done before in my life. Before, there had seemed to be no real reason for struggling beyond the effort for daily bread. Now there was a chance at that other that Jesus meant when He said we could not live by bread alone.

I have fought and kicked and fasted and prayed and cursed and cried myself to the point of existing. It has been like being born again, literally. Just "knowing" has meant everything to me. Knowing has pushed me out into the world, into college, into places, into people.

Part of what existence means to me is knowing the difference between what I am now and what I was then. It is being capable of looking after myself intellectually as well as financially. It is being able to tell when I am being wronged and by whom. It means being awake to protect myself and the ones I love. It means being a part of the world community, and being alert to which part it is that I have joined, and knowing how to change to another part if that part does not suit me. To know is to exist: to exist is to be involved, to move about, to see the world with my own eyes. This, at least, the Movement has given me.

The hippies and other nihilists[5] would have me believe that it is all the same whether the people in Mississippi have a movement behind them or not. Once they have their rights, they say, they will run all over themselves trying to be just like everybody else. They will be well fed, complacent about things of the spirit, emotionless, and without that marvelous humanity and "soul" that the Movement has seen them practice time and time again. "What has the Movement done," they ask, "with the few people it has supposedly helped?" "Got them white-collar jobs, moved them into standardized ranch houses in white neighborhoods, given them nondescript gray flannel suits?" "What are these people now?" they ask. And then they answer themselves, "Nothings!"

I would find this reasoning—which I have heard many, many times from hippies and nonhippies alike— amusing if I did not also consider it serious. For I think it is a delusion, a cop-out, an excuse to disassociate themselves from a world in which they feel too little has been changed or gained. The real question, however, it appears to me, is not whether poor people will adopt the middle-class mentality once they are well fed; rather, it is whether they will ever be well fed enough to be able to choose whatever mentality they think will suit them. The lack of a movement did not keep my mother from wishing herself bourgeois in her daydreams.

There is widespread starvation in Mississippi. In my own state of Georgia there are more hungry families than Lester Maddox would like to admit—or even see fed. I went to school with children who ate red dirt. The Movement has prodded and pushed some liberal

---

[5] nihilists—those who totally reject established laws and institutions.

senators into pressuring the government for food so that the hungry may eat. Food stamps that were two dollars and out of the reach of many families not long ago have been reduced to fifty cents. The price is still out of the reach of some families, and the government, it seems to a lot of people, could spare enough free food to feed its own people. It angers people in the Movement that it does not; they point to the billions in wheat we send free each year to countries abroad. Their government's slowness while people are hungry, its unwillingness to believe that there are Americans starving, its stingy cutting of the price of food stamps, make many Civil Rights workers throw up their hands in disgust. But they do not give up. They do not withdraw into the world of psychedelia. They apply what pressure they can to make the government give away food to hungry people. They do not plan so far ahead in their disillusionment with society that they can see these starving families buying identical ranch-style houses and sending their snobbish children to Bryn Mawr and Yale. They take first things first and try to get them fed.

They do not consider it their business, in any case, to say what kind of life the people they help must lead. How one lives is, after all, one of the rights left to the individual—when and if he has opportunity to choose. It is not the **prerogative**[6] of the middle class to determine what is worthy of aspiration. There is also every possibility that the middle-class people of tomorrow will turn out ever so much better than those of today. I even know some middle-class people of today who are not all bad.

What good was the Civil Rights Movement? If it had just given this country Dr. King, a leader of conscience, for once in our lifetime, it would have been enough. If it

---

[6] **prerogative**—special right, power, or privilege.

had just taken black eyes off white television stories, it would have been enough. If it had fed one starving child, it would have been enough.

If the Civil Rights Movement is "dead," and if it gave us nothing else, it gave us each other forever. It gave some of us bread, some of us shelter, some of us knowledge and pride, all of us comfort. It gave us our children, our husbands, our brothers, our fathers, as men reborn and with a purpose for living. It broke the pattern of black servitude in this country. It shattered the phony "promise" of white soap operas that sucked away so many pitiful lives. It gave us history and men far greater than Presidents. It gave us heroes, selfless men of courage and strength, for our little boys and girls to follow. It gave us hope for tomorrow. It called us to life.

Because we live, it can never die.

QUESTIONS TO CONSIDER

1. What effect did Martin Luther King, Jr., have on Alice Walker?

2. How does Walker counter the argument that those helped by the movement end up becoming members of the complacent middle class?

3. What did the Civil Rights movement "give" to Alice Walker and others?

Reflections on Martin Luther King, Jr.

On April 4, 1968, Martin Luther King, Jr., was assassinated by a white man in Memphis, Tennessee. King's death touched off a wave of riots in America's cities. When they subsided, the African-American community had to come to terms with the loss of one of its greatest leaders. In 1986, a national holiday was named after King. In the following selections the Chicago journalist Mike Royko reflects on what caused King's murder, and Ralph Abernathy, one of King's closest friends and colleagues, writes a letter to his departed friend.

Millions in His Firing Squad

by Mike Royko

FBI agents are looking for the man who pulled the trigger and surely they will find him.

But it doesn't matter if they do or they don't. They can't catch everybody, and Martin Luther King was executed by a firing squad that numbered in the millions.

They took part, from all over the country, pouring words of hate into the ear of the assassin.

The man with the gun did what he was told. Millions of bigots, subtle and obvious, put it in his hand and assured him he was doing the right thing.

It would be easy to point at the Southern redneck and say he did it. But what of the Northern disk-jockey-turned-commentator with his slippery words of hate every morning?

What about the Northern mayor who steps all over every poverty program advancement, thinking only of political **expediency**,[1] until riots fester, whites react with more hate, and the gap between races grows bigger?

Toss in the congressman with the stupid arguments against busing. And the pathetic women who turn out with eggs in their hands to throw at children.

Let us not forget the law-and-order-type politicians who are in favor of arresting all the Negro prostitutes in the vice districts. When you ask them to vote for laws that would eliminate some of the causes of prostitution, they babble like the boobs they are.

Throw in a Steve Telow or two—the Eastern and Southern European immigrant or his kid who seems to be convinced that in forty or fifty years, they built this country. There was nothing here until he arrived, you see, so that gives him the right to pitch rocks when Martin Luther King walks down the street in his neighborhood.

They all took their place in King's firing squad.

And behind them were the subtle ones, those who never say anything bad but just nod when the bigot throws out his strong opinions.

---

[1] **expediency**—adherence to self-serving means.

He is actually the worst, the nodder is, because sometimes he believes differently but he says nothing. He doesn't want to cause trouble. For Pete's sake, don't cause trouble!

So when his brother-in-law or his card-playing buddy from across the alley spews out the racial filth, he nods.

Give some credit to the most subtle of the subtle. That distinction belongs to the FBI, now looking for King's killer.

That agency took part in a mudslinging campaign against him that to this day demands an investigation.

The bullet that hit King came from all directions. Every two-bit politician or incompetent editorial writer found in him, not themselves, the cause of our racial problems.

It was almost **ludicrous.**[2] The man came on the American scene preaching nonviolence from the first day he sat at the wrong end of a bus. He preached it in the North and was hit with rocks. He talked it the day he was murdered.

Hypocrites all over this country would kneel every Sunday morning and mouth messages to Jesus Christ. Then they would come out and tell each other, after reading the papers, that somebody should string up King, who was living Christianity like few Americans ever have.

Maybe it was the simplicity of his goal that confused people. Or the way he dramatized it.

He wanted only that black Americans have their constitutional rights, that they get an equal shot at this country's benefits, the same thing we give to the last guy who jumped off the boat.

So we killed him. Just as we killed Abraham Lincoln and John F. Kennedy. No other country kills so many of its best people.

---

[2] **ludicrous**—laughable; absurd.

A week ago Sunday night the president said he was quitting after this term. He said this country is so filled with hate that it might help if he got out. Four days later we killed a Nobel Peace Prize winner.

We have pointed a gun at our own head and we are squeezing the trigger. And nobody we elect is going to help us. It is our head and our finger.

My Last Letter to Martin
by Ralph David Abernathy

Martin,

I miss you and it has been just a few days. I thought I would write you a short letter. It is probably more for my good than it is for yours. I hope it will not be too long before you read it. In Heaven I know you have so much to do, so many people to see. And I know many of them have already been looking and waiting for you. It wouldn't surprise me Martin, if God didn't have a special affair just to introduce his special activist black son to so many others like you that have gone on ahead. I know you wouldn't believe that could happen but then you did not understand how wonderful you are. . . .

Martin, go from the throne and find the Rev. George Lee, that stalwart hero who could barely read and write, who was shot down on the streets of Belzoni, Miss., simply because he wanted to vote. Check with Medgar Evers, who was shot down by mean and cruel white men, who thought they could turn us around by taking the life of this young man. Check with William Moore, another casualty in Alabama. And then Jimmy Lee Jackson, who died on the battlefield of Alabama. Oh, I wish you would look up Mrs. Viola Liuzzo, a white woman who was killed, you remember, on Highway 80;

and then check with Jonathan Daniels, a young theological Catholic student who died in Haynesville, Ala., down in Lowndes County, standing up for the rights of black people. James Reeb should be seen also, Martin. For James Reeb, a Unitarian minister, was beaten to death when he came to march for us in Selma. And don't forget Michael Schwerner and Andrew Goodman and James Chaney. You remember those three freedom fighters that they killed in Mississippi and buried their bodies beneath an earthen dam. Express our thanks to them. And then, Martin, don't forget the four little innocent girls who died in a Sunday School class in the 16th Street Baptist Church in Birmingham. They've been waiting to hear from us. Give them a good and complete report. And tell them that you left your people on your way. And we're determined that we ain't gonna let nobody turn us around.

And then, Martin, find Frederick Douglass, that great and marvelous human personality who lived in even more difficult times than we live today. Check with Nat Turner, and Marcus Garvey, for they, too, are heroes in our crusade. And oh, I wish that you would pause long enough at the mansion that is occupied by Abraham Lincoln, the man who freed us from physical bondage here in this country. Then, Martin, we owe a great debt of gratitude to John Fitzgerald Kennedy who less than five years ago, young as you were, brilliant as you were, filled with new ideas as you were, was shot down and killed as you were in cold blood by a mean, vicious and angry society. And don't forget Malcolm X. Look for Malcolm X, Martin. Remember our God is a loving God and he understands things we don't think that he understands. Malcolm may not have believed what we believe and he may not have preached but he was a child of God and he was concerned about the welfare of his people. And then, Martin, please do not forget about all of those who died across Alabama,

Mississippi, Louisiana, Chicago, and New York, and all other places where men have died for the liberty and justice of other men. Martin, it may seem like a big order, but if you find one of them, he will know where the rest are. And he will take you to them. I know that they have founded the grand international company of freedom fighters, and can't wait to introduce you to take over the final hours.

A man on Hunter Street said, "I envy the way that he died. He will be with so many who have died like he did. . . ."

It was early in the morning on December 2nd when I received a telephone call from E. D. Nixon, a Pullman porter, who told me how Mrs. (Rosa) Parks had been jailed, fingerprinted and mugged like a common criminal. He said to me that something ought to be done because this woman only wanted to sit down on the bus. And she refused to give her seat to a white man. But, before doing anything, I checked with you, Martin. Upon your suggestion, I went into action, began organizing the ministers, calling meetings. And from that day until now, our lives have been in action together. I remember how we talked together about who should be the leader of the new movement. You had not been in Montgomery very long. You were just out of the seminary and some people wanted me because they knew me. And I was president of many organizations in Montgomery. And I could have forced myself to be the leader. But I never, as you know, Martin, wanted to be the leader. I only wanted to stand with you, as Caleb stood with Moses.

From the grand action of the Montgomery movement, our lives were filled with the action of doing God's will in village, hamlet and city. We used to talk theology and then we learned to do theology. It was great. It has been great, Martin. Remember Gee's Bend down in Wilcox County, Ala.? Remember that day we stopped at a little filling station and bought jars of pickled pig's feet and some skins in Mississippi because they would not serve us at a restaurant. Remember, Martin, they wouldn't let us eat downtown? But our staff in that little crowded black man's country store had a fellowship, a kononia, together. We had a purpose and we had a universal sense of love that they did not have downtown. Some of my experiences with you will never be forgotten. You will recall how we went to Greensboro, N.C., when the sit-ins broke out, and how we sat in, in order that black men might stand up all over the world. You remember the Freedom Rides and how we were incarcerated and how we were forced to spend the night in the First Baptist Church in Montgomery with thousands of our followers while angry mobs stood on the outside. You remember the Albany movement and how Police Chief [Laurie] Pritchett and his forces tried to turn us around, and a divided Negro community became disgusted and despondent? You said to me, "Ralph, we must go on, anyhow." You remember Bull Connor brought out his vicious dogs, his fire engines and his water hoses and tried to stop us in Birmingham. But it was you, Martin, who said to me, "Ralph, don't worry about the water because we've started a fire in Birmingham that water can't put out."

You will recall Savannah, Ga., and how we went there to the aid and rescue of Hosea Williams. Hosea is still with me and he has promised to be to me, Martin, what I tried to be to you. You remember the March of Washington, when more than 250,000 Americans and people from all over the world came to hear you talk about "I Have a Dream"? You remember Danville, Va., and how they put us in jail? You remember St. Augustine, Fla., and Hoss Manuei when he said that he did not have any evil vices whatever? He did not drink liquor, he did not chase after women, he did not smoke. His only hobby was beating and killing [racial epithet].

But we knew how to deal with Hoss and we changed him from a Hoss into a mule. You remember how we worked on Bull Connor and changed him from a bull into a steer? You remember how we marched across Edmund Pettus Bridge in Selma and the state troopers lined across upon the orders of Gov. George Wallace and said that we could not pass. But we kept on marching. And when we got there, it opened up, like the Red Sea opened up for Moses and his army. You remember how Mayor [Richard] Daley tried to stop us in Chicago. But we would not let him turn us around.

My dear friend, Martin, now that you have gone, there are some special thoughts that come to me during this Lenten season. There are so many parallels. You were our leader and we were your disciples. Those who killed you did not know that you loved them and that you worked for them as well. For, so often, you said to us: "Love your enemies. Bless them that curse you and pray for them that despitefully use you." They did not know, Martin, that you were a good man, that you hated nobody. But you loved everybody. They did not know that you loved them with a love that would not let you go. They thought they could kill our movement by killing you, Martin.

QUESTIONS TO CONSIDER

1. According to Mike Royko, almost every American was in some way responsible for the assassination of Martin Luther King, Jr. What does he mean?

2. What message does Ralph Abernathy most want to give to Martin Luther King, Jr.?

3. Which of these two selections had a more profound effect on you? Explain why.

New Leaders

Malcolm X Black Muslims being harassed by the police. Malcolm X stands in the center holding up a newspaper decrying racism.

▲

Stokely Carmichael The leader of SNCC, Stokely Carmichael, speaks about Black Power at a conference at the University of California, Berkeley.

Revolutionary Poster A poster supporting the Black Panthers, the radical political party founded by Bobby Seale.

▼

▲

Martin Luther King, Jr., Assassinated The headline of *The Washington Post* for April 5, 1968, tells of King's murder by a white man in Memphis.

The Washington Post

The Weather · FINAL

91st Year · No. 123 · SATURDAY, APRIL 6, 1968 · Phone 223-6000 · 10¢

6000 Troops Rushed to District;
4 Dead in Day of Looting, Arson

Johnson Cancels His Trip

Joint Session Sought Monday On Civil Rights

1000 Arrested; Over 350 Injured; Curfew Imposed

Federal troops, wearing gas masks and carrying rifles, arrive at 13th and H Streets nw, where firemen battle a store fire.

▲

Rioting The front page of *The Washington Post* describes the riots that swept across the United States after Martin Luther King, Jr., was assassinated.

▲
America Was Murdered Last Night A march is held in honor of Martin
Luther King, Jr., and to protest the racism that led to his death.

Recollections

Four Poems

BY LANGSTON HUGHES

*Langston Hughes (1902–1967) was one of the leading writers of
the Harlem Renaissance in New York in the 1920s. By the 1950s,
he had become one of America's best-known writers and probably
the most influential African-American writer. His poetry followed
the changes in African-American life, and his last collection,* The
Panther and the Lash *(1967), traced the trajectory of the Civil
Rights movement. The following poems are from that collection, all
written in Hughes's unique style.*

"Words Like Freedom"

There are words like *Freedom*
Sweet and wonderful to say.
On my heartstrings freedom sings
All day everyday.

There are words like *Liberty*
That almost make me cry.
If you had known what I know
You would know why.

"Birmingham Sunday"

(SEPTEMBER 15, 1963)

   Four little girls
Who went to Sunday School that day
And never came back home at all
But left instead
Their blood upon the wall
With spattered flesh
And bloodied Sunday dresses
Torn to shreds by dynamite
That China made **aeons**[1] ago—
Did not know
That what China made
Before China was ever Red at all
Would redden with their blood
This Birmingham-on-Sunday wall.

---

[1] **aeons**—an immeasurably long period of time.

Four tiny girls
Who left their blood upon that wall,
In little graves today await
The dynamite that might ignite.
The fuse of centuries of Dragon Kings
Whose tomorrow sings a hymn
The missionaries never taught Chinese
In Christian Sunday School
To implement the Golden Rule.

Four little girls
Might be awakened someday soon
By songs upon the breeze
As yet unfelt among magnolia trees.

Freedom

Freedom will not come
Today, this year
Nor ever
Through compromise and fear.

I have as much right
As the other fellow has
To stand
On my two feet
And own the land.

I tire so of hearing people say,
Let things take their course.
Tomorrow is another day.
I do not need my freedom when I'm dead.
I cannot live on tomorrow's bread.
   Freedom
   Is a strong seed
   Planted
   In a great need.
   I live here, too.
   I want freedom
   Just as you.

Daybreak in Alabama

When I get to be a composer
I'm gonna write me some music about
Daybreak in Alabama
And I'm gonna put the purtiest songs in it
Rising out of the ground like a swamp mist
And falling out of heaven like soft dew.
I'm gonna put some tall tall trees in it
And the scent of pine needles
And the smell of red clay after rain
And long red necks
And poppy colored faces
And big brown arms
And the field daisy eyes
Of black and white black white black people
And I'm gonna put white hands
And black hands and brown and yellow hands
And red clay earth hands in it

Touching everybody with kind fingers
And touching each other natural as dew
In that dawn of music when I
Get to be a composer
And write about daybreak
In Alabama.

QUESTIONS TO CONSIDER

1. Is the speaker of "Birmingham Sunday" mostly angry or
   mostly sad? Support your answer.

2. What is the poet's message in "Freedom"?

3. What kind of "daybreak" is Hughes describing in "Daybreak
   in Alabama"?

from

A Time to Speak, A Time to Act

BY JULIAN BOND

*As a student at Morehouse College in Atlanta, Georgia, Julian Bond
(1940–) became involved in the sit-ins shortly after they started
in 1960. The next year, Bond was one of the founders of the Student
Nonviolent Coordinating Committee and served as one of its
leaders until 1965 when he ran for the Georgia State Assembly.
After he was elected, the assembly denied him office, ostensibly
because of his opposition to the Vietnam War. In 1966, Bond won
another election, and the U.S. Supreme Court unanimously upheld
his right to serve. Bond was a member of the Georgia Legislature
for thirteen years, working to promote integration from within the
system. In 1972, Bond published A Time to Speak, A Time to Act
which described his role in the Civil Rights movement and how he
felt about its successes and failures.*

W. E. B. Du Bois[1] correctly predicted that the problem of the twentieth century would be the problem of the color line.

With those words, he summed up the crisis that has primarily occupied men and nations and has become the first order of business for millions of oppressed peoples. Racism, the root of the crisis, is as old as the world itself. Internationally, the world's white minority has consistently exploited the resources of the colored majority of the world's population, and has continued to refuse to share the wealth and power it has gained in this way.

Here in the United States the struggle has been taken to the streets of most cities in the country, both violently and nonviolently. It broke out, for a time, on almost every college campus.

It was one part of the struggle that inspired Cuban cane cutters to overthrow a dictator and Vietnamese peasants to resist, ultimately successfully one hopes, through the bitter years, the attempts of outsiders to dominate their homeland. It is also part of the struggle that inspires Alabama sharecroppers to risk their lives in order to have a chance at controlling their destiny, a chance to vote, to find a decent job, to secure a good education for their children.

Dr. Du Bois believed that scientific and rational study of the problems of race and class would yield rational and logical solutions; civilized men, or educated men, are supposed to solve their problems in a civilized manner. That, at least, is what many of us have believed.

But the problems of the twentieth century are so vast, and the resistance to change has been so great, that many have quite naturally been tempted to seek uncivilized solutions. The problems include the poisoning of

---

[1] W. E. B. Du Bois (1868–1963)—African-American educator and writer.

the air and water; the rape of the land; the new colonialization of peoples, both here and abroad; the new **imperialism**[2] practiced by Western democracy; and the continuing struggle of those who have not against those who have.

At the birth of what was to become the **colossus**[3] called the United States, rational and educated men believed that civilization, stretched to its highest order, had begun. Building on a heritage of revolution, expressing a belief in the equality of most, if not all, men, this new democracy was to be the ultimate elevation of men's relationships, one to the other, and a new beginning of decency between nations.

Civilization, as it was then defined, included imposing limitations on war between nations; encouraging the spread of industrialization; the civilizing of so-called heathen elements, these being Indians and blacks; and the harnessing of nature for the benefit and pleasure of man. It was believed generally that man's better nature would triumph over his base desire to conquer and rule and make war, and that intellect, reason, and logic would share equally with morality in deciding man's fate.

Of course it has not been so. Man still makes war; he still insists that one group **subordinate**[4] its wishes and desires to another; he still insists on gathering material wealth at the expense of his fellows and his environment.

Men and nations have grown increasingly arrogant, and the classic struggle of the twentieth century continues, ever accelerating. The educated peoples of this world have enslaved the uneducated; the rich have

---

[2] **imperialism**—the imposing of power and authority over the politics and economics of others.

[3] **colossus**—something huge and important.

[4] **subordinate**—treat as having less value or importance.

dominated the poor; the white minorities have crushed the nonwhite peoples of the globe.

This revolutionary nation—revolutionary two hundred years ago—has become counterrevolutionary. This country, which has visited death on hundreds of thousands of Indochinese, has also found the arrogance to ignore the centuries of pleading for justice from her own domestic colony, the blacks. While these pleadings are dismissed, the central and final issue of the twentieth century comes to the fore, and violence is done to the notion that men can solve their problems without . . . violence. We need to discover just who is and who isn't violent in America. . . .

Yet an **antidote**[5] to that violence exists, an antidote that began with Denmark Vesey and Nat Turner, was given impetus by Du Bois and the Niagara Movement, and was spurred on by Martin Luther King, Jr., plus thousands of nameless fighters for freedom.

However, movements are not built on the helpful motions of a few, but by the determined actions of the mass. The chance at power comes in this country not in seizing a dean, but in seizing a welfare office; from organizing a strike of domestic workers; from beginning the arduous process of transferring strength and power from those who have it to those who do not.

This is not easy work. It is not easy because no one wants to do it. In an era of doing your own thing, no one wants to work with and for those whose thing is simply winning and maintaining the right to live. It means more than just the commitment of summer soldiers, although any soldiers are welcome in an understaffed army. It will require serious and systematic allocations of time and energy and resources.

---

[5] **antidote**—something that counteracts.

It will require that rhetoric be turned into action, that schoolbook knowledge be applied to street situations, that theories be turned into practice.

It will require that politics comes to mean people and their problems, and not just elections and candidates.

It will require that we build a movement strong enough to take over in a peaceful and orderly fashion; or to seize control, following the example of those who now exercise control.

That suggests there will be no peace. The oppressed of this land will not let peace prevail until they are given power or until they are destroyed by it.

When the day of judgment comes, we shall each have to add up our marks, and those who sat idly by and did nothing until that day shall be the first to go. But it will eventually consume us all. As the old spiritual says, "God gave Noah the rainbow sign, no more water, the fire next time."

This means, in our terms, the kind of commitment from young people that kept the South in **ferment**[6] in the heady days of the early 1960's. It is the kind of commitment that may take over the dean's office one day, but then the welfare office the next; the kind of commitment that will mean year-round participation in a new politics, a people's politics, a politics that will insure a choice, and not just an echo, at the top of the ballot.

And it will require that each of us keep in mind a prophecy written by the late Langston Hughes[7]—that dreams deferred do explode. For if this dream is deferred much longer, then an explosion certainly will come.

---

[6] **ferment**—in an agitated or intensely active state.

[7] Langston Hughes (1902–1967)—African-American writer and poet (see page 216).

Du Bois later enlarged his remark—that the problem of the twentieth century would be the problem of the color line—to include the problem of the have-nots pitted against the haves.

Sixty-five years ago, he wrote a personal credo that if adopted by those in power would be a beginning in the struggle to eliminate the problem:

> I believe in God who made of one blood all races that dwell on earth. I believe that all men, black and brown and white, are brothers, varying, through Time and Opportunity, in form and gift and feature, but differing in no essential particular, and alike in soul and in the possibility of infinite development.
>
> Especially do I believe in the Negro race; in the beauty of its genius, the sweetness of its soul, its strength in that meekness which shall inherit this turbulent earth.

QUESTIONS TO CONSIDER

1. According to Julian Bond, what is the major problem of the twentieth century?

2. Bond says it's time to act. What kind of action is he talking about?

"Common Ground"

FROM A SPEECH BY JESSE JACKSON

Jesse Jackson (1941–) was an active protester during the Civil Rights movement. Throughout the 1970s and 1980s, Jackson continued to fight for African-American equality. In 1984 and 1988 he ran for the Democratic Party nomination for President of the United States, the first African American to mount a serious candidacy for our nation's highest office. In 1988, he gave a speech at the Democratic Convention that reminded his audience how much difference the Civil Rights movement had in fact made.

Tonight we pause and give praise and honor to God for being good enough to allow us to be at this place at this time.

When I look out at this convention, I see the face of America—red, yellow, brown, black and white, we're all precious in God's sight—the real Rainbow Coalition. All of us, all of us who are here, think that we are seated, when we are standing on someone's shoulders. Ladies and gentlemen, Mrs. Rosa Parks. The mother of the civil rights movement. . . .

My right and my privilege to stand here before you has been won—won in my lifetime by the blood and the sweat of the innocent.

Twenty-four years ago, the late Fannie Lou Hamer and Aaron Henry—who sits here tonight, from Mississippi—were locked out in the streets of Atlantic City, the head of the Mississippi Freedom Democratic Party. But tonight, a black and white delegation from Mississippi is headed by Ed Cole, a black man from Mississippi, 24 years later.

Many were lost in the struggle for the right to vote. Jimmy Lee Jackson, a young student, gave his life. Viola Luizzo, a white mother from Detroit, called "[racial epithet] lover," and brains blown out at point-blank range. Schwerner, Goodman and Chaney—two Jews and a black—found in a common grave, bodies riddled with bullets in Mississippi. The four darling little girls in the church in Birmingham, Alabama. They died that we might have a right to live.

Dr. Martin Luther King lies only a few miles from us tonight. Tonight he must feel good as he looks down upon us. We sit here together, a rainbow, a coalition— the sons and daughters of slavemasters and the sons and daughters of slaves sitting together around a common table, to decide the direction of our party and our country. His heart would be full tonight.

As a testament to the struggles of those who have gone before; as a legacy for those who will come after; as a tribute to the endurance, the patience, the courage of our forefathers and mothers; as an assurance that their prayers are being answered, their work has not been in vain, and hope is eternal; tomorrow night my name will go into nomination for the presidency of the United States of America.

We meet tonight at the crossroads, a point of decision. Shall we expand, be inclusive, find unity and power? Or suffer division and impotence?

We come to Atlanta, the cradle of the Old South, the **crucible**[1] of the New South. Tonight there is a sense of celebration because we have moved, fundamentally moved from racial battlegrounds by law, to economic common ground, tomorrow the challenge to move to moral higher ground.

Common ground! Think of Jerusalem, the intersection where many trails met. A small village that became the birthplace for three great religions: Judaism, Christianity and Islam. Why was this village so blessed? Because it provided a crossroads where different people met, different cultures, different civilizations could meet and find common ground. When people come together, flowers always flourish, the air is rich with the aroma of a new spring.

Take New York, the dynamic metropolis. What makes New York so special? It's the invitation of the Statue of Liberty—"Give me your tired, your poor, your huddled masses who yearn to breathe free." Not restricted to English only. Many people, many cultures, many languages—with one thing in common, the yearn to breathe free. Common ground!

Tonight in Atlanta, for the first time in this century, we convene in the South. A state whose governors once stood in schoolhouse doors. Where Julian Bond was denied his seat in the state Legislature because of his conscientious objection to the Vietnam War. A city that, through its five black universities, has graduated more black students than any city in the world. Atlanta, now a modern intersection of the New South.

Common ground! That's the challenge to our party tonight. Left wing. Right wing. Progress will not come through boundless liberalism nor static conservatism, but at the critical mass of mutual survival. Not a boundless liberalism nor static conservatism, but at the critical

---

[1] **crucible**—a gathering of powerful intellectual, social, economic, or political forces.

mass of mutual survival, but it takes two wings to fly. Whether you're a hawk or a dove, you're just a bird, living in the same environment, in the same world. The Bible teaches when lions and the lambs lie down together, none will be afraid, and there will be peace in the valley.

It sounds impossible. Lions eat lambs; lambs sensibly flee from lions. Yet even lions and lambs can find common ground. Why? Because neither lions nor lambs want the forest to catch fire. Neither lions nor lambs want acid rain to fall. Neither lions nor lambs can survive nuclear war. If lions and lambs can find common ground, surely we can as well as civilized people. . . .

The greater good is the common good. As Jesus said, "Not my will, but thine be done." It was his way of saying there is a higher good beyond personal comfort or position. The good of our nation is at stake. Its commitment to working men and women, to the poor and the vulnerable, to the many in the world. . . .

Common ground. Easier said than done. Where do we find common ground? At the point of challenge. This campaign has shown that politics need not be marketed by politicians, packaged by pollsters and pundits. Politics can be a moral arena where people come together to find common ground.

We find common ground at the plant gate that closes on workers without notice. We find common ground at the farm auction where a good farmer loses his or her land to bad loans or diminishing markets. Common ground at the school yard where teachers cannot get adequate pay, and students can't get a scholarship, and can't make a loan. Common ground at the hospital admitting room, where somebody tonight is dying, because they cannot afford to go up to a bed that's empty waiting for somebody with insurance to get sick. We are a better nation than that. We must do better.

Common ground. What is leadership if not present help in a time of crisis? So I have met you at the point of challenge. In Jay, Maine, where paper workers were striking for fair wages. In Greenfield, Iowa, where family farmers struggle for a fair price. In Cleveland, Ohio, where working women seek comparable worth. In McFarland, California, where the children of Hispanic farmworkers may be dying from poisoned land—dying in clusters with cancer. In the AIDS hospice in Houston, Texas, where the sick support one another, too often rejected even by their own parents and friends. Common ground.

America is not a blanket, woven from one thread, one color, one cloth. When I was a child growing up in Greenville, South Carolina, and grandmomma couldn't afford a blanket, she didn't complain and we didn't freeze. Instead she took pieces of old cloth—patches— wool, silk, gaberdine, croker sack—only patches barely good enough to wipe off your shoes with. But they didn't stay that way long. With sturdy hands and a strong cord, she sewed them together into a quilt, a thing of beauty and power and culture. . . .

. . . They wonder why does Jesse run. They see running for the White House. They don't see the house I'm running from.

I have a story. I wasn't always on television. Writers wasn't always outside my door. When I was born late one afternoon, August the 8th in Greenville, South Carolina, no writers asked my mother her name. . . . You see, I was born to a teenage mother who was born to a teenage mother.

You see, I understand. I know abandonment and people being mean to you and saying you're nothing and nobody and can never be anything. I understand.

Jesse Jackson is my third name. I am adopted. My grandmother gave me her name. My name was Jesse Burns until I was 12. So I wouldn't have a blank space she gave me a name to hold me over. I understand when nobody knows your name. . . .

I wasn't born in a hospital. Mama didn't have insurance. I was born in the bed in a house. I really do understand. Born in a three-room house. Bathroom in the back yard. Slop jar by the bed. No hot and cold running water. I understand. Wallpaper used for decoration, no, for a windbreaker. I understand.

I am a working person's person. I wasn't born with a silver spoon in my mouth. I had a shovel programmed for my hand. My mother was a working woman. Too many days she went to work early, with runs in her stockings. She knew better, but she wore runs in her stockings so my brother and I could have matching socks and not be laughed at at school. I understand.

At 3 o'clock on Thanksgiving Day, we couldn't eat turkey, because Mama had to pass somebody else's turkey at 3 o'clock. . . . I really do understand. Every one of these funny labels they put on you, those of you who are watching this broadcast tonight in the projects, on the corners, I understand. They call you outcast, low-down, you can't make it, you're nothing, you're nobody, subclass, underclass.

When you see Jesse Jackson, when my name goes in nomination, your name goes in nomination. I was born in the slum, but the slum was not born in me. And it wasn't born in you. And you can make it. Wherever you are tonight, you can make it. Hold your head high, stick your chest out, you can make it. It gets dark sometimes, but the morning comes. Don't you surprise.

Suffering breeds character. Character breeds faith. In the end, faith will not disappoint. You must not surrender. You may or may not get there just because you are qualified, but you hold on and hold out. We must never surrender. America will get better and better. Keep hope alive. Keep hope alive. Keep hope alive on tomorrow night and beyond. Keep hope alive.

I love you very much. I love you very much.

QUESTIONS TO CONSIDER

1. What kind of common ground is Reverend Jackson looking for?

2. What helps Jackson understand the agony of the poor and downtrodden?

3. Do you think Jackson's speech inspired his listeners to "keep hope alive"? Explain your response.

ACKNOWLEDGEMENTS

11 Recollection of Reverend Joe Carter from *Who Speaks for the Negro?* by Robert Penn Warren, Random House, 1965.

23 From *Coming of Age in Mississippi* by Anne Moody. Copyright © 1968 by Anne Moody. Used by permission of Doubleday, a division of Random House, Inc.

34 From *Thurgood Marshall: Justice for All* by Roger Goldman with David Gallen, Carroll & Graf Publishers, Inc., 1992.

51 Recollection of Rosa Parks from *My Soul is Rested* by Howell Raines. Copyright © 1977 Howell Raines. Used by permission of Putnam Berkley, a division of Penguin Putnam Inc.

53 Recollection of Yancey Martin from *My Soul is Rested* by Howell Raines. Copyright © 1977 Howell Raines. Used by permission of Putnam Berkley, a division of Penguin Putnam Inc.

59 James Meredith's Statement from *Three Years in Mississippi* by James Meredith, Indiana University Press, 1966.

62 From *Coming of Age in Mississippi* by Anne Moody. Copyright © 1968 by Anne Moody. Used by permission of Doubleday, a division of Random House, Inc.

69 "Revolution in Mississippi" from *Black Protest* by Joanne Grant, edit. Copyright © 1968 by Ballantine Books. Reprinted by permission of Ballantine Books, a Division of Random House Inc.

72 "Letter from a Mississippi Jail" by Robert Moses, from *Documentary History of the Civil Rights Movement,* ed. Peter B. Levy, Greenwood Press, 1992. Copyright © 1992 by Peter B. Levy. Reproduced with permission of GREENWOOD PUBLISHING GROUP, INC., Westport, CT.

82 from *Freedom Ride* by James Peck. Reprinted with the permission of Simon & Schuster, Inc. Copyright © 1962 by James Peck, copyright © renewed 1990 by the Executors of the Estate of James Peck.

96 From "Letter from a Birmingham Jail" by Martin Luther King, Jr. Reprinted by arrangement with The Heirs to the Estate of Martin Luther King, Jr., c/o Writers House Inc. as agent for the proprietor. Copyright 1963 by Martin Luther King, Jr., copyright renewed 1991 by Coretta Scott King.

109 "I Have a Dream" by Martin Luther King, Jr. Reprinted by arrangement with The Heirs to the Estate of Martin Luther King, Jr., c/o Writers House, Inc. as agent for the proprietor. Copyright 1963 by Martin Luther King, Jr., copyright renewed 1991 by Coretta Scott King.

126 Testimony of Fannie Lou Hamer before the Credentials Committee of the Democratic National Convention, August 22, 1964, Atlantic City, NJ.

129 From "Deeper than Politics: The Mississippi Freedom Schools," by Liz Fusco in *Liberation,* November 1964.

131 *Freedom School Poetry,* SNCC, 1965.

134 From *Three Lives for Mississippi* by William Bradford Huie.

141 Willie Bolden's Recollections from *My Soul is Rested* by Howell Raines. Copyright © 1977 Howell Raines. Used by permission of Putnam Berkley, a division of Penguin Putnam Inc.

144 From *Selma, Lord, Selma,* by Webb, Nelson and Sikora, 1980, The University of Alabama Press. Used by permission.

158 *The Fire Next Time* excerpted from "Down at the Cross: Legion from a Region in My Mind." © 1962 by James Baldwin. Copyright renewed. Originally published in *The New Yorker.* Collected in *The Fire Next Time,* published by Vintage Books. Reprinted by arrangement with the James Baldwin Estate.

175 "The Black Revolution" by Malcolm X from *Malcolm X Speaks.* Copyright © 1966, 1989 by Betty Shabazz and Pathfinder Press. Reprinted by permission.

186 "What We Want" by Stokely Carmichael from *Stokely Speaks: Black Power Back to Pan-Africanism,* Random House, 1965. Originally titled, "What We Want."

194 "The Civil Rights Movement: What Good Was It?" from *In Search of Our Mothers' Gardens: Womanist Prose,* copyright © 1967 by Alice Walker, reprinted by permission of Harcourt, Inc.

202 "Millions in His Firing Squad" by Mike Royko. *Chicago Sun-Times,* April 9, 1968. Reprinted with special permission from the Chicago Sun-Times, Inc. © 1999

217 *Collected Poems* by Langston Hughes. Copyright © 1994 by the Estate of Langston Hughes. Reprinted by permission of Alfred A. Knopf Inc.

222 *A Time to Speak, A Time to Act* reprinted with permission of Simon & Schuster, Inc. from *A Time to Speak* by Julian Bond. Copyright © 1972 by Julian Bond.

227 "Common Ground" from a speech by the Rev. Jesse Jackson before the 1988 Democratic National Convention, July 1988.

Photo Research Diane Hamilton

Photos Courtesy of the Library of Congress and the National Archives.

Every effort has been made to secure complete rights and permissions for each selection presented herein. Updated acknowledgments, if needed, will appear in subsequent printings.

Index